Training for What?
Labour Perspectives on Job Training

André Beckerman, Julie Davis,
Nancy Jackson (editor),
D'Arcy Martin, Doug Olthius,
David Robertson, Jim Turk

Canadian Cataloguing in Publication Data

Main entry under title:

Training for what : labour perspectives on job-training

(Our schools/our selves monograph series ; no. 11)
ISBN   0-921908-12-1

1. Employees, Training of – Canada. I. Jackson, Nancy S., 1946–

HF5549.5.T7J33 1992   658.3'1243   C92–095745–5

This book is published by Our Schools/Our Selves Education Foundation, 1698 Gerrard Street East, Toronto, Ontario, M4L 2B2 .

For subscribers to *Our Schools/Our Selves: a magazine for Canadian education activists*, this is issue #26, the second issue of volume 4.

The subscription series Our Schools/Our Selves (ISSN 0840–7339) is published 6 times a year. Publication Mail Registration Number 8010. Mailed at Centre Ville, Montréal, Québec.

Design and typesetting: Tobin M^{ac}Intosh.

Cover photo: Lisa Sakulensky.

Our Schools/Our Selves production: Eleanor Brown (Managing Editor), Nancy Jackson, Loren Lind, Doug Little, Bob Luker, Tobin M^{ac}Intosh, George Martell, Mary Ann O'Connor, Susan Prentice, Satu Repo, Harry Smaller.

Printed in Canada by La maîtresse d'école inc., Montréal, Québec.
Copyright © Our Schools/Our Selves Education Foundation
November 1992.

Preface

Training is clearly on the agenda of public policy and political life. The reasons are many. Training is central to current management initiatives for the restructuring of work. It is also critical for politicians, as a substitute for a coherent industrial strategy. Most important, training has a powerful impact on the lives of working people, but it can be either friend or foe, depending on how it is done.

The papers in this book look at training as a tool of political struggle in the workplace. They show how it can contribute to skill recognition, to safe and satisfying working conditions, to career progression, and to building a more democratic vision of working life. They identify issues and avenues for activism both inside and outside the current collective bargaining framework.

The appendices provide major OFL (Ontario Federation of Labour) and CLC (Canadian Labour Congress) policy documents and samples of contract language for several affiliates which may serve as a useful reference.

Some of the papers that appear here were originally part of an Ontario Federation of Labour Conference on Training. A number of other issues discussed at this conference are not reflected in these pages, such as the still-fragile social bargaining that is ongoing around the federal and provincial training boards, or training for the unemployed and underemployed. All of these issues are important to the growing debates about policy and the politics of training, and we hope they will be the topic of future volumes.

Meanwhile, we hope the present book will serve as a resource in many workplaces. It may help us think about training that is good for workers as well as for employers. It may also help us fight for training as a collective right, not just as an individual benefit.

Toronto, November 1992 *Nancy Jackson*

MYTHS ABOUT TRAINING

1. More training is necessary because we are moving to a high tech future.

Almost every projection on future jobs — including those done by the federal government — points to the following six occupations as having the fastest growth over the coming years: secretaries and stenographers, janitors, cashiers and tellers, office clerks, waiters, and truck drivers. The government studies concluded that most of these future jobs can be filled by people now unemployed or those needing little training.

2. Highly-trained high-technology jobs mean higher wages.

Many high tech industries — like computer chips, computer processing, and auto production — have moved to low-wage countries like South Korea or Taiwan. Within Ontario, there are many high-tech companies with relatively low wages. Higher wages are not just technologically determined but depend on unionization and social and political factors.

3. A more highly trained workforce will mean jobs in Canada.

It is not true that more training is the key to jobs in Canada. The reason for Canada's particular economic structure is complex and simply increasing training will not change our economic structure. Training is not the critical factor explaining our economic dependency on resources, assembly, and U.S. technology.

4. A lack of training has hindered the development of the Canadian economy.

The problem has not been inadequate skills but the under-utilization of existing skills: workers with skills being laid off; workers forced to work part-time because no full-time jobs exist; educated workers doing menial jobs because there are no openings in their fields.

5. Good planning for specific skill shortages is a priority.

Detailed planning for the future is not possible in a changing, unplanned economy. The alternative is to provide broad skills training so that workers (and companies) will have the flexibility to adapt their abilities to specific uses as the need arises.

6. Training is not a controversial issue.

Aside from the question of how much training should be done, there are fundamental disagreements about who is to benefit from the training, and about the kind of workplace and society the training is meant to reinforce.

Labour's agenda is for training that equips workers to have more control over their jobs and their work lives; builds on workers' existing capabilities; prepares workers for what they want and need to know now and in the future; puts workers in a better position to shape that future and that starts eliminating job discrimination based on gender, race or ethnicity.

The employers' training agenda is to make workers willing and able cogs in the corporate machine.

7. Training is a good thing.

Not all training is good. It can be harmful. Just as the educational system has made many workers doubt their abilities and competence, bad training can weaken self-confidence, scare people away from opportunities they could pursue, reinforce stereotypes and past discrimination, and undermine critical abilities and initiative.

This is why the labour movement wants the ability to shape training so it meets the needs of workers.

8. Multiskilling will provide greater job security.

There is no evidence for this. Jobs are vulnerable as long as employers have the unrestricted right to close plants and relocate work.

Since multiskilling often undermines traditional trades, it may even weaken job security. Traditional trades are portable whereas employer-designed multiskilled work is usually not portable. Multiskilling can make workers more dependent on the whim of the current employer.

An addendum to the OFL policy paper on
Education and Training in Appendix I.

Contents

Preface   *iii*
   Nancy Jackson

Introduction   *1*
   If "Training" Is The Answer,
   What Is The Question?
   Jim Turk

Chapter One   *8*
   Training On The Job?
   You've Got To Be Kidding ...
   Julie Davis

Chapter Two   *18*
   Corporate Training Syndrome
   David Robertson

Chapter Three   *29*
   The Meaning Of Multiskilling
   David Robertson

Chapter Four   *43*
   Collective Bargaining And Training
   Doug Olthius

Chapter Five 50
Fighting For Training:
Fighting For A Future
André Beckerman

Chapter Six 66
Unions And Training In Ontario
D'Arcy Martin

Chapter Seven 76
Training Needs:
An Objective Science?
Nancy Jackson

Appendices 85
Union Policies And Contract
Language On Job Training

Appendix I 87
OFL: Education And Training

Appendix II 104
CLC: Training And U.I.

Appendix III 123
CAW: Collective Agreements
On Training

Appendix IV 132
OPSEU: Sample Clauses
On Training

Appendix V 148
CUPW: Training Agreement
with Canada Post

Introduction

If "Training" Is The Answer, What Is The Question?
Jim Turk

Training Has Become Fashionable

After years of neglect, business and governments have discovered training. They have even elevated it to being the key to our economic future. Canada's efforts in training, so they claim, will determine whether we become an economic powerhouse or are consigned to the dustbin of history.

Rarely have the corporate and government elite so affirmed the importance of workers' skills.

This training refrain is being sung by the federal government, all provincial governments, the Business Council on National Issues, the Canadian Manufacturers' Association, the Chamber of Commerce, the Ontario Premier's Council, the Council of Ontario Universities and many others.

They contrast the importance of training with how little training is being provided currently. They launch volleys at the educational system for having prepared workers so badly. They bemoan the state of illiteracy in Canada. In almost evangelical terms, they implore us to take up the gospel of training.

What Is Really Going On

Too bad things are not as they appear.

First things first. Surprisingly, when you ask workers if they can do their jobs well, you get an almost uniform answer — "Yes." When you then ask whether they were trained by their employer to do the jobs — the most common answer is "No." Try this out yourself on your friends.

This suggests how little employer training is provided — a fact confirmed by numerous national and provincial surveys. It also suggests something far more important: most people must be good learners. Most people have taught themselves (with help from their co-workers) how to do their jobs and do them well!

With all the talk about no training, the horrors of our educational system, and Canada's widespread illiteracy, it is amazing that anyone is competent at their work, much less almost everyone.

"Ah, but ... the future will be different," you will undoubtedly hear if you talk this way to the experts. "No longer will workers be able to get by. In the high-skill, high tech, high-value-added future, most people will need post-secondary education!"

Who says so? you may ask. Well the federal government says so. Learned business economists say so. Self-promoting experts say so.

But there is very little to back up their claims. The most sophisticated job forecasts of any western industrialized country are issued by the U.S. Bureau of Labor Statistics. Their forecasts for some years have been remarkably consistent — over the next decade, most new jobs will be toward the bottom of the skill range: cashiers, janitors and cleaners, truck drivers, waiters, nurses aides and attendants, and salespeople.

The Canadian Occupational Projection Service (COPS) comes to similar conclusions.

"Ah, but ... even these jobs will involve using computers so people will have to be literate," is the usual response at this point in a discussion.

That's true enough, but the skills have been programmed into the computers so the workers can be thoroughly deskilled.

Just look at McDonald's — one of the really high tech workplaces. Everything is programmed so that an untrained workforce, with minutes of training, working short shifts, with lots of employee turnover, can turn out a remarkably consistent product that meets the employers' specifications almost flawlessly.

Rather than an exception, McDonald's use of technology to deskill work is the model toward which most employers are striving. Such an approach cuts labour costs and allows increasingly sophisticated production to be shifted to locations with little skilled labour.

As American writer and teacher, Douglas Noble, asked at an Ontario Federation of Labour conference on education:

> "Why, in an increasingly high tech work world, that ... displaces and deskills more and more workers every week, do corporate pronouncements endlessly promote sophisticated education and training as the key to corporate competitiveness and worker survival?"

The most common answer is that the deskilling is a response to an insufficiently skilled workforce. More emphasis on training, according to these folks, will reverse the deskilling. There is no reason to believe such a claim.

Training Is Not The Key To A Better Ecomony

Quite frankly, those who see education and training as determining our economic future have the situation backward.

Public and private investments in education and training are hardly going to be the major factor determining multinational capital's decisions about investment in Canada. Sure, an appropriately trained labour force is an element in corporate decision-making, but there is nothing that Canada can do to be distinctly stronger than many other countries.

Rather than education and training being a cause, it is the result of economic decisions. Emphasis on education and training is more likely to flow from a vibrant and fully-industrialized economy than be the factor to bring it about.

Better economic policies may do more to promote an emphasis on education and training than anything else.

None of this is news to anyone who has thought seriously about the relation of training to the economy. Training is not and cannot be a major factor in bringing about a better economy. But, for a variety of reasons, many ignore this fact.

Why The Sudden Interest In Training?

For some, emphasis on training is a way to blame the victims of Canada's badly managed economy.

Guided by neo-conservative economic policies for more than a decade, Canada's economy has suffered a decline unparalleled since the Depression. The economic medicine of deregulation, privatization, free trade, high real interest rates and tight monetary policy has sent Canada spiralling into depression and has thrown close to two million into unemployment and underemployment. Canada has lost close to a fifth of its manufacturing base and shows little prospect of cyclical recovery in the foreseeable future. Rather than face the devastating mistake of its economic policies, Canada's government and corporate leaders have chosen to imply that a big share of the blame lies with workers by suggesting workers' lack of skills is the problem and training is the answer.

They do this in the face of clear contrary evidence. The World Economic Forum and the International Institute for Management Development's *World Competitiveness Report*, that ranks the world's industrialized countries on competitiveness, puts Canada in the top five in terms of workers' skills. But such evidence does not slow down those intent on blaming workers for Canada's economic mess.

For others, the emphasis on training is an understandable and common-sense answer to a bewildering economic situation. Unable to grasp the larger issues of the economy, they can find hope in the simple prescription of more emphasis on training.

Often this is music to workers' ears. It recognizes two things that workers have always known. One is that their skills (both acknowledged and unacknowledged) are necessary to make the economy run. The second is that their employers have never provided the training workers deserve.

Labour wants training not because we are doing so badly, but because it is an educational right to which workers are entitled.

For yet others, talk of training is a way to camouflage the reality of corporate power and control. Over the past several decades, there has been an unprecedented concentration of capitalist power in the hands of a very small number of giant corporations. The largest 100 corporate enterprises (far less than 1/10 of one percent of all corporate enterprises) in Canada account for 56 percent of all assets and 45 percent of all corporate profits.

Giants like General Motors, IBM, General Electric and Exxon have annual sales figures that are larger than many countries' gross national products.

It is reassuring to pretend that minor differences in educational and training support and policies among Western industrialized countries can affect the behaviour of these giants. The limited power of nation-states in the face of these massive economic titans raises serious and frightening questions. Rather than address these, some find comfort in pretending that national education and training policies can make a measurable difference in corporate investment decisions among industrialized countries.

Why Labour Wants Training

Whatever the reasons for the new-found corporate interest in training, they are very different than labour's.

While training is important for labour, we are very clear that it is not a substitute for an economic strategy for full-employment — a strategy that will produce secure, well-paying jobs. Nor is it a substitute for labour adjustment programs that provide income support and other necessary social assistance while helping people find alternative work.

We see two objectives for training.

One is helping develop a more productive economy. It is this objective that is so frequently overstated by those who see training as the keystone of economic development. Training is nothing more than a tool, one among many, in building a more productive economy. But our special commitment to training goes well beyond that economic objective.

Training is part of the educational entitlement of working people — an entitlement to education that not only helps them as employees but also as people. It is an entitlement that should be available to employed workers, displaced workers, and those wanting to enter or re-enter the labour force.

Labour's View Of Good Training

For the educational and economic objectives to be realized, the issue is not just the amount of training but the nature of the training.

In dealing with the amount, we feel that there will only be sufficient training when employers are obligated to provide training. This would be most adequately achieved by the introduction of an employer training levy. This measure would require all employers to pay a certain percentage of payroll to provincial training boards that would use the money to fund training programs.

Under such a scheme, responsible employers would get their investment back while those who chose not to train (relying on those who do) would at least have to help cover the costs of others' training. Systems like this have provided the backbone for the best European training systems in the past.

Equally important is the nature of training that is provided. To meet our economic and educational objectives, skills training must be developmental. Skills must be taught in ways not simply limited to a particular job. The participant should come away from the experience better able to take on a variety of tasks and more confident as a learner.

It is essential that training incorporate the practices of good adult education, starting with what the participants already know and with what they want to know. It should respect the many abilities people bring to training and encourage questioning, discussion and participation.

Training should help people have more control over their jobs and their work life, learn more about individual and collective rights and reflect the workers' identification of skills needs.

Employed workers should receive training entitlements at full pay, accumulated by all workers in guaranteed and measurable terms — such as days per worker per year.

Accessibility to training for displaced workers and those entering or re-entering the labour force should be assured by government provision of adequate income support as well as necessary social support services such as child care and counselling.

Conclusion

One of the ironies in the discussions about training is that everyone speaks of its necessity, while having very different objectives.

Labour's framework is set out clearly in the Ontario Federation of Labour and Canadian Labour Congress policy documents in Appendices I and II to this book.

The articles in the book explore different aspects of training issues from a labour perspective. We hope this volume will broaden the discussion of training among working people and build support for training that strengthens workers, helps overcome past discriminatory practices in the workplace, and lets workers have more control over their jobs.

Jim Turk is Director of Education for the Ontario Federation of Labour.

Chapter One

Training on the Job?
You've Got to be Kidding...

Julie Davis

I have been asked to tell you a story. It's a story that many of you are going to know very well from your own lives. It's about the skills I have needed and the training I have received in the many jobs I've held during my working life. Telling my own story like this has made me notice a lot of things about jobs and training that I never thought about before. I hope that hearing about my experiences will suggest new ideas for you too.

But before I get to the story, there are five basic things I think we need to keep in mind in any discussion of training:

> First, most of the job training in this country is provided by co-workers. I am going to talk more about this point in a minute.

> Second, while more and more employers are stressing the importance of training, precious few of them are providing any formal or informal training themselves. I am sure your experience shows this as well as mine.

> Third, there is not necessarily a relationship between what employers call 'skill' and what you need to know in order to do your job.

Fourth, there is no necessary relationship between training and skill.

Fifth, and I think most importantly, the real issue for us is control over our work. Training doesn't always help us achieve this goal.

For all these reasons, I have a lot of trouble with what the business community is telling us about training these days. They claim that training is the key to Canada's economic future. They claim that our ability to attract industry and to maintain a healthy economy is dependent on the training of workers. Well, I think they have got the cart before the horse. Training follows from a strong economy, it does not create one.

All you have to do is look at what is happening in Canada today. Over 400,000 good — and by that I mean well-paid — manufacturing jobs have left Canada since the free trade agreement was signed. These jobs did not leave Canada because there were too few well-trained workers here. They left because employers could get cheaper labour in the American sun belt or in Mexico. And just as importantly for the corporations, they do not have to worry about environmental legislation, workers' compensation regulations, health and safety or those other kinds of restrictions that would stop them from doing what they want. The reality is that all the training programs in the world would not have kept those jobs here in Canada. Just like the absence of training programs in Mexico or the United States has not stopped the companies from choosing to move there.

The same thing is clear for the public sector. Work is being contracted out, jobs are being privatized, workers are being cast aside and our economy is in shambles. The popularity of privatization and contracting out has nothing to do with training.

I think we need to very clear about this point. New training programs for workers in the public sector will neither save their jobs nor create new ones. This is always important to keep in mind whenever you hear training being offered as the solution to your troubles.

I wanted to start with these reminders because I feel it is really important as trade unionists to put training in perspective. Training is not the cure-all. Training is not the key to saving our economy or to eliminating poverty. To do those things we need to cancel the free trade deal, increase the minimum wage, stop privatization and contracting out, make it harder for plants and facilities to close down, and have the federal government put some money back into job creation so there are jobs that people can train for. Those are our principal economic tasks.

So, training to create a more skilled workforce is not important to us because it will save the economy; it will not. But — and it's a big but — if it's done right, training can help empower workers. It can help us take more control over our jobs and our work lives. Only certain kinds of training can do this. It's not the kind I have ever received, and I am sure that my experience in that regard is not unique. In fact, I received very little training from any employer for whom I have ever worked. But now I am getting ahead of my story.

A Whole Labour Council

Over the years, I have had quite a variety of jobs in many different kinds of workplaces and in many different sectors of the economy. In fact, some of my friends tease me and say "Julie could be a whole labour council all by herself" because of the number of different jobs I have had and the number of different unions that I have belonged to over the course of my working career.

I started when I was about eleven baby-sitting for neighbours' kids. After that I had several waitress jobs, only two of which are memorable. I spent a year as a car hop at the Shake and Burger restaurant in Brantford, Ontario. What's so memorable about that? Well, they stayed open all one winter. It is pretty unique being a car hop in the winter time in Ontario! I was also a waitress in a place called Marcel's restaurant, also in Brantford. Marcel was famous only because he was Robert Goulet's best man at his first marriage. Everyone has long since forgotten the bride's name, but that was Marcel's claim to fame.

Over the next few years I held a variety of jobs in the Brantford area. I worked at Hayes stationery store. I built small motors at Robinson Myers, a factory that no longer exists in that community. I worked at Heintzman's piano factory. This was in the days when pianos were still built in Ontario; I don't think they are even built in Canada any more. I was a carpet inspector at Harding Carpets, another factory that has become history due to the free trade agreement. I was an assembly line worker at Johnson's Wax.

For a while, I worked in a machine shop, though I can't for the life of me remember either the name of the machine shop or what it was that I did there. I can still picture what it looked like and where it is in Brantford. I could probably drive back to Brantford and take you there, but that is all that I can remember about it. Then I went to work at Crane Canada where they make plumbing fixtures. This was as close to a sweat shop as a brand new plant could get. No windows, an air circulation system that did not work very well, particularly in the summertime, and a plating shop where there was almost no ventilation. On hot humid days in the summer you could not see one end of the plating shop from the other. That was not because the room was big but because of unventilated fumes. This was in the days before I knew very much about health and safety. I would not work there today.

I then did a lot of freelance clerical work for a number of unions, including IUE (International Union of Electrical Workers), and the NDP (New Democratic Party) and then became a secretary for CUPE (Canadian Union of Public Employees), eventually becoming a staff rep with CUPE and then moving on to work as an officer of the OFL (Ontario Federation of Labour).

So, all in all, I have had quite a variety of experiences in my working life. But there are common elements running through all of these different jobs. For most of these jobs there was absolutely no formal training. Usually a co-worker showed me, sometimes for half-an-hour, sometimes for half a shift. Sometimes the foreman or the leadhand would show me how to operate the machine or what-have-you. But for the most part I was left on my own to learn how to do all of the things that were important for these jobs.

Now there were a couple of exceptions. For instance, I had really good on the job training to be a baby-sitter. That's because I was the oldest of six children and my mother taught me how to baby-sit from an early age! She taught me well, because she needed my help to survive.

As a secretary the only on the job training I'd had was high school typing and the rest of it I faked. I pretended I had not worked on "that kind" of Gestetner machine before and would ask somebody to show me how it worked. Or I would say we did not have "this kind" of postal meter where I had worked, and someone showed me how it worked. I picked up what I was shown and, other than getting Gestetner ink all over myself and the documents a couple of times, I did not do too badly. I also had to learn to balance the demands of working for several bosses. That is one of the most important things that secretaries have to do.

When I became a CUPE staff rep, I was taken away to Ottawa for a week of orientation. But this only happened after I had been on the job for a whole year! The first thing they taught us in orientation was how to fill out our expense forms. Well, as anybody knows the very first thing you learn when you go on the job is how to fill out your expense forms! However it was nice to spend a week in Ottawa. My first assignment was a number of local unions in the Lindsay area, near Peterborough. To equip me for that assignment, I was given a box of files and was told, "To get to Lindsay, take the 401 to Highway 35/115 and go north. Take the Lindsay cutoff, continue right straight into the middle of town to the main street, and that's where everything is." To be fair, I don't want to malign my previous employer (from whom I'm still on leave). They did eventually provide arbitration training, and today they do a lot more training. They have realized the importance of making sure that staff people are well informed, so staff representatives today get a lot more training than I did.

Learning That's Taken For Granted

I also realized, when I stopped to think about it, that a lot of learning took place during the course of all those jobs. But it is really hard for us to see that, because so much of it is taken for granted. When I was a sales clerk my co-workers showed me how to stock the shelves, how to work the cash register, how to rotate stock, how to keep track of which companies got the corporate discount, and all those things.

In the plating shop, it was important that I placed the part to be plated on the rack properly so that the chrome took and it was not shadowed in any way. I also had to learn how to stay away from the sulphuric acid bath and how to jump away if a piece fell off a rack and into the bath. If it splashed, sulphuric acid would give you a nasty burn. At the piano factory, my job was putting screws into the hammer. I had to line it up properly. If I didn't, the hammer would crack and break. And I was expected to do that in a reasonably fast way, because they had quotas.

As a waitress, I learned a lot by trial and error. At Marcel's Coffee Shop, I learned how to balance two or three plates at once, especially after I spilled a grilled cheese sandwich into a customer's lap. At the time I was just glad that it was not blueberry pie. Eventually the other staff showed me how to put plates down without having the food slide off the plate.

At Robinson Myers where I was building small motors, I had to learn how to do spot welding. I learned the importance of wearing your hairnet over all of your hair after I set my hair on fire while soldering some wires. There is a reason you have to wear hairnets in some of the factories and it's not because they make you look so horrible. It's because they stop worse things from happening to you.

So when I think about it, it is clear to me that there was no relationship between what employers recognized as skills and what I needed to know in all these workplaces. Most of these jobs were treated as unskilled, and most of us who did these jobs thought of them as not requiring skills. Usually we still think this way. But it's just not true. There is a lot we need to know to do any job and only some of those things are treated as skills. As Harry Braverman argued more than 20 years ago, what gets treated as a skill is a political issue, and work traditionally done by women is less likely to be labelled as skilled.

For instance, I have talked a little bit about a clerical job. Well, there is a lot of skill needed to be a good secretary. Yes, it is important to be able to type or take shorthand, be able to answer the telephone properly and take down good messages. But it is also important to be able to cover diplomatically for the person for whom you are working. This happens frequently, like when your boss is out and hasn't told you where she/he is going, and her boss (or someone else important) is calling and asking, "Where the hell is so and so," and "Why isn't she here?" Then it's your job to cover, saying "I know he/she is somewhere important, I just seem to have lost the details!"

Then there is the problem of balancing multiple demands. Most of the secretaries I am familiar with, including those at the OFL, have to work for two or three different people. And so you have to balance the demands of those different personalities and learn to set priorities. All of those things are pretty important; they make the difference between being good or bad at your job.

I could give you a similar list of things that I had to know for each of the other jobs that I have had. But what's important is the realization that learning on the job happens so much as a matter of course that whatever we learn we tend not to see as skills or as things that we have learned at all. We see them as just part of the job. I want to thank Jim Turk for helping me to see this, because when we first talked about it, I kept saying that, well, I hadn't really learned anything. I just did the jobs, you know. I worked in the factory, I built the motors, or I worked in the plating shop or what have you. It was only through sitting down and talking about each of those different jobs that I began to realize that yes in fact there are a lot of skills required; it is just that nobody ever recognized them. Employers don't recognize them, society tends not to recognize them. So we tend to not recognize them ourselves. But just try asking a professional person (or an academic!) and see how quickly most of them can rattle off what they have had to learn for their jobs.

Tricky Issues

So my main point here is that the issues of skills and training are very tricky. Many of the things that we need to know to do our work are not treated as skills. And many other things that we need to have some control over at work are being taken away. Yet we are being told at the same time that our jobs are getting more skilled. Employers who have never provided training (and still resist doing so) are telling us that training is the most important element in our economic future. What are they actually offering us and why? Well, these are important questions, and ones that I think we need to grapple with very carefully.

We want training because we want more control over what we do at work. But we also recognize that there are very many different types of training, and just because something is called 'training' doesn't mean that it is necessarily good for us. There are many kinds of training that we don't want. We don't want training modeled on obedience training for dogs: "Sit, heel, roll over, play dead." Yet, this is precisely what some employers have in mind when they advocate training. Training that instructs the workers how to do what he or she is told to do, and to do so willingly. As a sign in one plant says, "Don't do it well, do it right."

We also don't want training that focuses on brainwashing us. Much of the so-called employer-based training aims at getting the worker to look at the world through the employer's eyes. The need to think of the workplace as a team where the boss is just another member. The need to remember the importance of profitability. The need to keep competitiveness at the forefront of our thoughts. And the need to forget what the employer calls "old fashioned" notions like worker solidarity. This is what David Robertson calls 'cultural training,' and to confuse it with skills training is, I think, a very serious mistake.

We also don't want training that's run in a way that makes us doubt our competence, weakens our self-confidence, ignores our abilities and our intelligence, or reinforces stereotypes and past discrimination. We have had enough of that in our lives. We don't want training that narrowly prepares us to do one job but fails to leave us any better off when that job changes or when we move to a better job.

So maybe we need to abandon the word 'training' altogether — reserve it for the teaching of pets. Instead, perhaps we should refer to what we want for ourselves as 'education.' I think that term comes closer to what labour has been fighting for. What we want is a way of learning that respects our abilities and draws on them. We want to learn things that will leave us stronger and better able to function effectively, not only at work but also outside the workplace. We want educational programs that are a vehicle for equality for women, for visible minorities, for native people and for disabled persons. Simply put, we want educational programs that strengthen us collectively as workers. We want educational programs in which our experience and knowledge shape the objectives and content of the programs. And most of all we want to participate in educational programs that put us more in control of our work.

The debate about what a 'skill' is or how we can define this term could go on forever. A hundred years ago it was a lot clearer. Skilled workers in those days were those whose knowledge and experience put them in control of their work. And what we have seen over the years, and increasingly today, is employers consistently trying to take that control away from us. They have reorganized workplaces, they've introduced new technologies, they've engaged in innumerable practices to assert their control over us and our work, and we have always found ways to fight back. Now they are getting more sophisticated. They are starting to talk like us. They are starting to acknowledge the importance of training. But we have to be very careful. We have to look at what they are saying and what they are doing. We can't afford to buy the myth that training is a good thing in itself. Some training can be very good and some of it can also be very harmful. And as workers we need to be clear about the difference. That's the reason that training has become a major policy area at the Ontario Federation of Labour with a statement adopted at the 1989 convention [see Appendix I].

So we need to respond to all this talk about training. We need to respond by saying, yes, but no. We want opportunities to learn, but not at any cost. We want programs that respect our abilities, recognize our skills, empower our voices in the workplace. We want training that builds stronger futures for ourselves and our unions as well as for our communities and our country. Only by working together and talking to each other will we find the way to achieve this kind of learning at work. This struggle has just begun.

Julie Davis is Secretary-Treasurer of the Ontario Federation of Labour.

Chapter Two

Corporate Training Syndrome
What we have is not enough & more would be too much
David Robertson

There is obviously more to training than corporate training for employed workers. But it is specifically these programs I want to talk about here. I'm going to take a look at employer training programs — and at what passes for training — for those of us who have jobs.

Specifically I have three objectives:

1. I want to provide some of the basic facts and figures which record the inadequacy of corporate training efforts. Answers to questions about who trains and who gets trained can help us make the case for a system that obligates employers and regulates training;

2. I want to make some observations about the nature of corporate training programs — Who do they serve? What do they teach? How do they train? Here the answers will outline the business training agenda and will underline the need for a labour agenda on training;

3. More tentatively, I want to question the meaning of 'skill' and raise some questions about the relationship between

training and skill. Then, I will end by talking about some principles that might help define from our perspective — what training is.

Before doing any of that, I want to make clear what training isn't. Training isn't an economic strategy, no matter how they dress it up. Neither is it a solution to unemployment. It is not an adequate response to economic restructuring, nor is it even the most effective way to ensure the welfare of individual workers. It will not guarantee future prosperity for our economy or our selves. In other words, training is not a substitute for our more traditional demands of full employment and a more democratic economy. When we start getting involved in training, it is important to keep these larger political issues in mind, so we don't lose our way.

Facts And Figures

In the last five years there has been a flood of reports on training. There have been federal studies and provincial studies. There have been taskforces and advisory councils, special commissions and bipartite committees all examining training. In the process we have heard a great deal about the new corporate training culture, about enlightened Human Resource strategies — I even had one manager tell me they weren't a factory anymore, they were a university! But what do we actually know about the extent of training?

The short answer is what we have always known. Companies don't train. To rely on employers to train us is as promising as counting on them to safeguard our health in the workplace or to voluntarily promote affirmative action and pay equity. But all these studies have given us some figures:

- Canadian business spends less than one half of 1 percent of its payroll on formal training programs. Let me put that in perspective. One half of 1 percent of payroll is not even half the U.S. level. And the U.S. level is considered a national calamity because it lags so far behind other countries.
- In Canada it has been estimated — on an economy-wide basis — that companies annually spend about $100 to $150 per employed worker on training. That means that com-

panies are probably spending more on cardboard than on training workers. It means, in a company of 500 workers, less is spent on training than on the salary of one middle level manager.

But even these figures actually overstate the commitment to training in Canada. First, because only one out of every three or four companies in this country actually has a training program. And second, because even amongst those companies with a program, training is unevenly distributed. We know from the studies and from our own workplaces that the overwhelming share of training goes to managers, administrators, and to non-bargaining unit professional and technical workers.

But let's be generous. Let's say that out of the $100 per employed worker I noted earlier, 25 percent is spent on training our brothers and sisters. That works out to about 1 cent an hour. In the Canadian Autoworkers, we have negotiated a higher contribution than that to our Paid Education Leave program. It's just not enough.

The unequal distribution of training isn't only a question of managers vs. workers. It is also a problem even within our own bargaining units. Let me use an example. Recently one of the Big Three auto makers finally supplied us with some hard data on training. In one plant the average training time per worker was just over 6 hours a year. However low, these averages still overstate the training available for some workers, because the figures combine both skilled trades and production. If you separate the figures out again, they show the skilled trades with about 19.5 hours of training and production workers with about 1.5 hours. This is not nearly enough for the trades and a bad joke on everyone else.

The data also suggests we have to distinguish between training budgets and expenditures. I recall being impressed by the headlines: "Company budgets $200 million for training over the next five years." But there is a difference between budgets and what is actually spent. In one large assembly plant, for example, the actual amount spent on training in 1989 was only 15 percent of what was actually budgeted. And for the first 5 months of 1990, the amount actually spent was less than 4 percent of what was budgeted.

So do we have answers to the questions about who trains and who gets trained? The answers aren't encouraging. The 1990 report of the Ontario Premier's Council under the Peterson government talks about a serious "training deficit" and it is clear that we have exactly that. But it is not a deficit that can be balanced by simply adding more training. Instead, we have to examine what really happens in the name of training.

Corporate Training

Most of what happens in training can be represented under two headings: One is training for cultural integration. The other is training around technical developments and new technology. Let's look at them one at a time.

Cultural Integration:

Companies today exert considerable effort trying to shape the attitudes of the workforce and influence the behaviour of individual workers. These could be called corporate identity programs. In fact, the major training programs General Motors has projected for the 1991–93 period are Human Relations/Communications and Problem Solving. When it comes to training, GM has a clear preference for "interpersonal skills" over "technical skills." GM calls it "cultural training."

Similarly, Northern Telecom talks about building "a strong corporate culture which encourages the workforce to accept the company's goals as its own." And McDonnell Douglas talks about a "supportive cultural environment." In fact, McDonnell Douglas has set a training target of 10 percent of base hours. Ten percent of base hours works out to about 200 hours a year. That is impressive! Very few companies set training targets at all, and even fewer would set them so high. But when we find out what is proposed for training, the urge to applaud evaporates. Out of a list of 15 examples of training, there is only one mention of job skills and only one mention of technology improvements. The rest of the list is filled with references to versatility training, human relations, problem solving, continuous improvement training, conflict management, team building and standardized work.

Training for cultural integration is not a way to restore the training deficit. Instead, its goals are to facilitate work reorganization, to generate narrowly-defined productivity improvements and to integrate workers into the value system of the company.

Technical Training:

How companies define their needs and responsibilities, especially around technical developments and new technology, can best be made by describing a series of six workplace situations.

- A worker in a marketing department is performing tasks on a computer using Lotus 1–2–3. The company knows that it is possible to know very little about Lotus and still be capable of functioning in the job. In fact, management expects the person to use only one screen of Lotus, and even then to know only how to call up that particular screen and fill in the appropriate blanks. In this office, Lotus was part of a completely new marketing system, but the logic of the system wasn't revealed to the workers and some of the basics of Lotus were actually concealed. The training provided was limited and instrumental. It consisted of a set of instructions of "how to do this and when to do that." Too often under the guise of "user friendly" technology, we end up being treated like idiots.

- In a different plant, the machine shop brought in a new Toshiba CNC — a complicated piece of equipment worth close to a million dollars. The training was 'catch-as-catch-can.' One person was able to look over the shoulder of those who installed the equipment, and when the installers left he was told, "Here is the equipment, this is what it does, read the manual."

- Workers in the planning department of an aerospace company had access to ongoing training. Whenever they had some additional time on their hands, they could go on line to a selection of pre-packaged courses provided by a major U.S. owned instructional corporation. This meant that in addition to working all day at their VDT screens, workers could now sit in front of them to get trained as well. The de Grandpre report of several years ago, called "Adjusting to Win," promoted this computer-based model of training. In fact, it talked about the tremendous opportunity that exists in such computer-based training techniques and it recommended using "the experience of industrial and military institutions ... as a model."

- In yet another plant, part of the purchase price of a new CMM, a computerized inspection system, included a vendor training package which provided training at the vendor's site for one person. When the person returned, the expectation was that he would train everyone else. But there was no time set aside for the training, and the demands of production still had to be met. In other words, workers in the same job get much different training and soon end up with different degrees of knowledge and confidence on the new technology.

- Recently you could get into the purchasing department as a trainee so long as you had some seniority. Once you were there you would be trained to do the job. Now the requirement is a certificate from the Purchasing Management Association of Canada (PMAC). The way you get the PMAC certificate is after hours and on weekends on your own time. Jobs are becoming more qualification-based because management is successfully writing credentials such as these into the job descriptions.

- Finally, there is the spokesperson for Toyota who summarized his company's training approach as, "We just try to keep it simple." By extension the point is this: simple jobs, simple skills, simple training, simple people. This approach may suit Toyota, but it's not good for workers.

So whether it is a new software package, a new CNC machine, a new type of skilled trade or whatever, the corporate approach to training is about the same. On the one hand provide only what is needed to make it operate, and on the other hand demand more credentials and qualifications for jobs we have been doing all along or could be doing given the chance.

Training And Skill

Unfortunately, training has joined a growing list of words that make me nervous. I call them company babble — words like "world class," "high technology," "multiskilling," "state of the art," "flexibility" and "teamwork." Part of the problem with these words is the relationship always implied between high tech, high skills, high wages and a highly trained workforce. And part of the problem is that once we automatically associate more training with higher skills, we risk losing sight of one important fact. That is, the way companies define skills and deliver training can actually degrade the content of our jobs. We can't afford to overlook this point.

Let me be specific. The CAW (Canadian Autoworkers) represents the agents who work in Air Canada Reservations offices. The jobs of reservation agents can be described by all the corporate babble words. They are "knowledge workers" in the "information age." Their jobs are "computer-based" and they work at "state of the art" workstations, accessing first one "data base" and then another. They are expected to provide "world class" service in a rapid succession of "customer interfaces." And they are "flexible" — able to respond rapidly to changing information and a constant stream of software enhancements. They are "multiskilled" workers. In addition to the keyboard skills, they are computer literate and their jobs require marketing skills as well as interpersonal skills.

Compared to most workers, these reservation agents are highly trained. At the entry level they are given six weeks of intensive training — in the classroom and on the floor. They are provided periodic training updates and refresher courses. And it is commonly accepted that it takes six months, a year, even two years to be proficient at the job. They have all the characteristics of the "high tech worker."

At the same time, these workers have jobs which are oppressively controlled and becoming more so. Management is forcing shorter call lengths and it is trying to standardize the actual conversations. The agents are forced to conform to performance standards that are rapidly tightening up around them. They are subjected to constant surveillance in the form of electronic measurement, regular call monitoring and managerial eavesdropping. It is not surprising that reservation agents have stress levels which are exceptionally high. How do we reconcile these two sets of characteristics? On the one hand we have a highly trained and computer-skilled workforce and on the other harassed workers and intensified work. The point is that we cannot separate the meaning of training from the content of our jobs, and we cannot separate skill levels from control over work. It takes more than just long hours of training to make a good job.

Look at our workplaces — we've got upskilling and deskilling; we have reskilling and multiskilling; we have generic skills and portable skills; and increasingly we hear talk of pay-for-skills. In such a context what does skill actually mean? It has become a buzz word that is really getting out of hand. Let me give you a nice example.

Recently, the Ontario Ministry of Skills Development gave me a copy of a document they commissioned entitled a Generic Workplace Competency Profile. This Generic Workplace Competency Profile was designed for entry level positions in the automotive parts industry. In the first few pages the document lists what are called "some desirable personal attributes" such as maturity, a team player, creative, punctual, respects property, has constructive thoughts, is adaptable, healthy, aware, self-motivated, self disciplined, loyal, literate, articulate and shows initiative by asking for additional jobs. (Would you want this person as a friend?) This is only a selection. The list is actually longer.

The rest of the document provides a detailed breakdown of what are called "skill sets" in a number of different categories like basic skills, technical skills, personal management skills. These so-called "skill sets" go on and on, page after page. I actually counted them. There are 195 skill items on the list. And as the document states, these are only the generic competencies; they do not include the job specific skill components.

Remember the document in question was constructed for an entry level position in the auto parts sector and was commissioned in order to help the ministry develop a training program. I was told by those responsible for the document that nothing like it had ever been done before. To which I replied that perhaps it was never done before because it simply isn't necessary. We don't need it! But the real point is that it is more than unnecessary, it is actually hazardous to working people. It elevates managerial expectations. It treats as 'objective' a process of defining needs on the job which lacks credibility because it deliberately excludes the union. It legitimates as "generic" and as "competency" a managerial wish list for the model corporate citizen, peppered with some reasonable technical issues.

Look at some of the skill items, like "interprets body language." My first thought was that it had something to do with maintaining the robots — but the previous skill item was "expresses body language." Here's another one. "Communicates with all levels of the organization on behalf of fellow employees." Remember this is an entry-level position. I can just see it. Shirley picks up the phone and calls Head Office. "Mr. President, me and the sisters want to have a word with you about the decision to shift steering wheel covers to Mexico!"

Then there are my favourite skill items: "describes the competitive nature of the business" and "explains variables affecting costs and profits." Somehow I doubt that the training on costs and profits would talk about Mulroney's high interest rate policy or about the amount of gross profits that flow in shareholder dividends or the amount that is siphoned off in intra-company transfers to head office. Instead, I think instruction would have a lot to do with "labour costs," "absenteeism," "idle time" and "waste." Training like this we don't need.

It is not enough that training is on the public agenda. It is not enough that we get some new structures, some new commitments and what looks like a new consensus on training. For years the labour movement has been arguing for "generic" skills. Now we have companies and government agreeing. But in the process, they are becoming the ones to defining what is meant by "generic."

Let me give an example. Recently, I saw a press release describing a new training initiative that involves labour, management and government. The press release said that money would be used to promote generic skills. Then it used as an example SPC (Statistical Process Control). But when did SPC become a generic skill? SPC involves understanding some mathematical concepts and being available to plot quality conformance graphs. But that doesn't make SPC a generic skill. Surely from a labour perspective we should be arguing that every worker has the right to achieve a grade 12 level in math. That would be a generic skill — it might even help companies introduce SPC, but that is not the goal. This interpretation would be a very different form of training.

A Labour Agenda

As part of our response to the issue of training — part of our effort to shift the debate to grounds more favourable to labour — it is necessary to think about what principles we would support. Our goal of developing a labour agenda on training can start with the following:

1. Training is a basic working right and an integral part of the job.
2. Training objectives and goals have to be developed in specific and measurable terms, such as hours per worker, and all workers must be guaranteed that training.
3. Training should be conducted during working hours and without production pressures.
4. The goals, content and delivery of training programs should be co-determined and should be based on the principles of adult education.
5. Training should be developmental. The programs should teach skills that go beyond a particular job or work area.
6. Training programs should be open to all workers, not just the youngest or the fittest, and special efforts should be made to use training as a vehicle for social equity.
7. Training should be geared to raising the level of skill of the entire workforce, not just selected occupations or selected areas.
8. Training should support and develop a worker-centred definition of skill and not be restricted to job performance or academic factors.

9. Training should support the development of good job design and technologies which respect the skills of the worker.

This list is only a start. There's way more to add and more work to be done to define our specific interests in training in different workplaces and differing circumstances. We need to continue working together on these issues — toward a training strategy that has as its signposts democratic rights and better jobs.

David Robertson is a national representative in the Research Department of CAW–Canada.

Chapter Three

The Meaning Of Multiskilling
David Robertson

There is a story I heard the other day about two behavioural psychologists, the stimulus-response types, who had met on a consulting job for a local firm. As the project proceeded they became attracted to each other and finally consummated their relationship. Afterwards, the more ardent of the two turned to the other and said: "It was great for you. How was it for me?"

When it comes to multiskilling, unlike the story, we know what it's like for us. But perhaps even more telling, I would argue that it isn't all that great for you either.

These are the two central points I want to make. First, there is very little in multiskilling, beyond the rhetoric, to recommend it to labour. Second, against its claims of securing time economies and achieving high machine utilization rates, we must balance the downside of shallow maintenance skills, dissatisfied workers, and diminished internal control of your own production processes.

It is clear that multiskilling has joined a growing list of workplace flexibility initiatives — in one shape or another it seems to be everywhere. The literature is chock-a-block with references to multiskilling and multicrafting. We hear about polyvalent workers and multifunctional workers, we hear about multipurpose training and cross-training, and we hear about hybrid skilled workers and versatile production workers.

Despite all this, I believe that the tales of success of multiskilling have been greatly exaggerated. The CAW (Canadian Autoworkers) has just completed a round of bargaining with the Big Three auto companies. In two of those negotiations the issue of multiskilling didn't even come up and in the third, there was an initial interest expressed by the company in "cross-training some apprentices." But when the union asked what it was the company wanted, it was never followed up.

I don't want to make too much of this. But I do want to argue that we have to resist a faddish enthusiasm, fuelled by tales from elsewhere, that encourage us to emulate work practices which, we are told, account for the competitive success of other companies or countries.

I think we must trust what we know about our own workplaces. Multiskilling is not some Rosetta Stone that can decipher the productivity code of our workplaces and infuse our work with new meaning.

Nor do I think it gets us very far to start from what has emerged as a prevailing orthodoxy that restrictive work rules and outdated shop floor practices are hemorrhaging the productive forces in our industry. Somehow through multiskilling, inflexible and outdated job demarcations are supposed to give way to a more rational job allocation.

We all know what happens. It's like the debate around classifications. Despite reports in the press, it is not simply the case that management demands fewer classifications while the unions defend the status quo. There are situations where it is the union asking for fewer classifications. In fact, in the recent Ford talks the union wanted to eliminate a number of classifications and Ford wanted to keep them on the book. Even when management pushes for fewer classifications it is quick to create new ones in order to build fences around special jobs it wants protected from posting and bumping provisions. In other words, we know that work rules are often situation specific and that every situation is complex. So, about multiskilling, my point is this: that neither orthodoxy nor faddish emulation will get us very far.

Any discussion of multiskilling needs a starting point. Ours is the central principle that a workplace should be an effective production system and at the same time an attractive place for human beings. Let me turn that around and look at it from the other side. We want good working conditions, more security and better job content for workers and a workforce that can provide a better and long term contribution to the productive capacity of our workplaces and our economy.

The question arises — does multiskilling take us in those directions?

I'm going to answer the question in two parts. First by discussing multiskilling in production work, and then by reviewing multiskilling in the trades.

Production

In production the new competitive agenda is reportedly to achieve a workforce which is flexible, cross-trained and multiskilled. There are three ways this most often gets expressed. One has to do with task variety, another with multi-machine minding, and a third involves the absorption of indirect duties.

I will take these in turn by referring to specific work situations.

Task Variety

Take an assembly line in a team concept auto plant. It could either be a feeder line like an instrument panel (IP) line or part of the main line that is the jurisdiction of a particular team. The example in Figure 1 below is a mechanically paced IP line which feeds the main assembly line in an auto plant. There are twelve stations on the line each with a fixed and consistent job cycle of about 2 minutes. Workers on the IP line are called multi-functional workers and they can and do rotate through a number of positions on the line. Despite the language of multiskilling their jobs conform to the following set of strictures.

1. Jobs must be broken down into small units of discrete tasks.
2. Each job must have a detailed definition so it can easily be reassigned.
3. The skill level required for each task must be limited so it can be quickly learned.
4. Each job must be balanced in terms of time. The operation time for each and every process on the line must be the same time.

5. Workers must be able and willing to do any job.

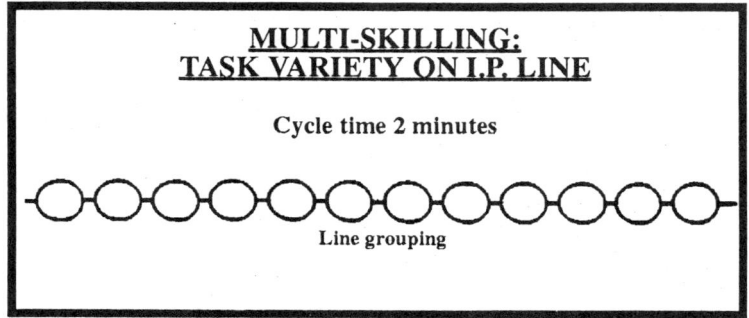

Figure 1

In other words this form of multiskilling is premised on rigidly prescribed routines and short cycle times.

We have had utility jobs in traditional plants where a person can do all the jobs in an area. But I see no evidence that we are trying to create workplaces full of utility people. Instead the concept of multiskilling is really a practice of multi-tasking.

It is possible to design factory jobs to require a broad range of worker skills but that isn't what multiskilling is about. Let's stick with the example of the IP build. In Figure 2 we have two

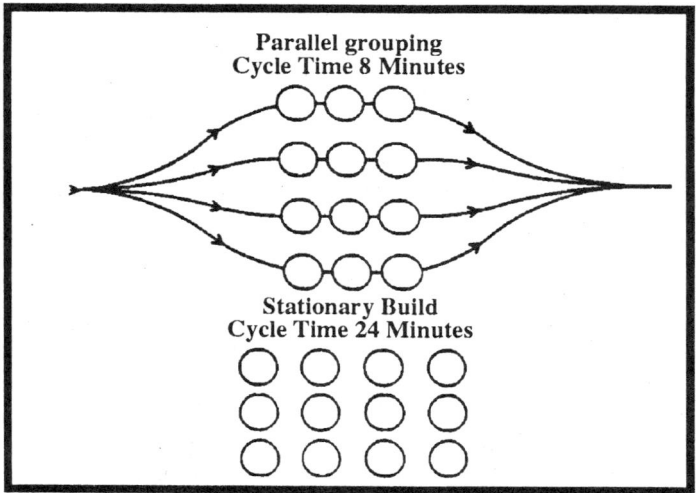

Figure 2

re-organized work settings: the first a parallel grouping and the other a stationary build work station.

Here we immediately see the prospect of longer work cycles, 8 minutes in the one case and 24 minutes in the other. The jobs have more task variety, workers have greater skills and more autonomy in terms of pacing, especially in the stationary build situation. These work situations would better approach a union's sense of multiskilling.

Multiple Machine Minding

In multiple machine minding, the goal is work intensity rather than skill development. People from Toyota use an overhead of a u-shaped line to talk about multiskilling. I've got the same overhead which I've taken from *The Toyota Production System* by Yasuhiro Monden, but I use it to talk about work intensity.

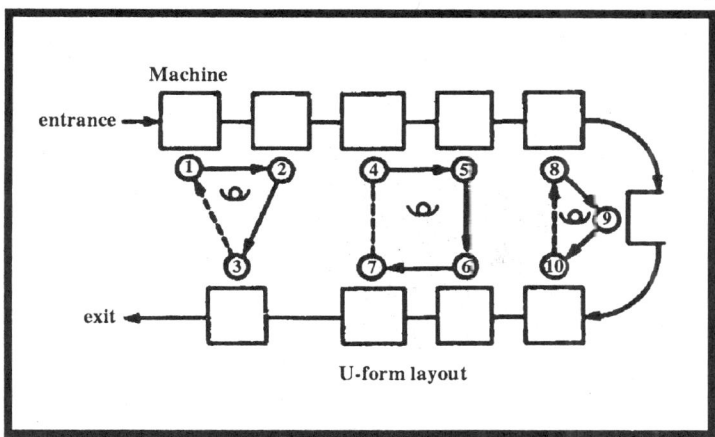

Figure 3

If a worker operates one machine why not two; if three machines, why not four? Figure 4 is reproduced from the CAMI Automotive Inc. training manual, the note which accompanies the diagram reads:

Each person must handle several processes —

For the operation time to be the same at each process, one operator should not work at only one process or one machine, since there would be waste from idle time. Therefore, it is necessary for each operator to work at more than one process and to handle various operations. People who say "I'm a lathe operator and can't do any other job" are not needed. We must have people who can handle a variety of operations within a certain range.

We must be multi-functional, not single-functional associates.

In multifunctional work situations to be capable of operating more than one machine means each operator is reduced to a rapid succession of loading and unloading tasks.

Figure 4

Absorption Of Indirect Functions

There is a difference in perception about job design between managers and workers. Obviously, where you are in an organization affects your perspective and your attitudes.

A case in point is the use of the slide line for circuit pack assembly in Northern Telecom. Slide lines are manual assembly lines for the serial and progressive build up of printed circuit packs. In one of our case studies a senior manager described the slide line jobs with the language of multiskilling and good job design. Slide line assembly jobs were referred to as *broader* jobs. We were told that they were not only *enlarged* but they were *enriched*. There was *more variety* in the job and people were doing *more on the job*. There was more responsibility, such as inspection and there was job rotation. Indeed, the jobs were held out as proof that the company was no longer "*hiring from the neck down*."

Workers' sense of those jobs was considerably different. The jobs were described as physically constrained and restricted. Workers referred to themselves as robots. An assembler inserts a few components and then manually slides the board on to the next person in the line. Rotation they said was a cruel joke: "Instead of putting six capacitors in, we can put six resistors in." Instead of increasing skill content of the job the slide line actually degraded the job content. The jobs were more boring, more repetitive and more stressful.

In fact, before the slide line was introduced, one assembler built the board from start to finish. Here we have a situation where multiskilling involves the denigration of existing skills — even while it is described in completely different terms.

Job Satisfaction

There is a story one of our staff reps tells about a meeting with Japanese trainers and supervisors at a new plant in Ontario. The discussion started with the differences between Japanese and Canadian workplaces and in particular, the differences between workers. In Japan, workers are multiskilled, engaged in broad jobs, given responsibility and authority and they are capable of doing many jobs, while in contrast, Canadian workers are limited to narrow, low-skilled, repetitive jobs. The point was made that Japanese workers are, as a result, more skilled than their Canadian counterparts and are more satisfied with their work. When it came time for the staff rep to respond he did so by describing his 16 or so years in an auto company. How he started as an assembler, moved to various other assembly jobs, spent some time in the paint shop, in stampings, then as a relief operator and finally ended up as an inspector. He turned to the Japanese and asked, "In your mind would that make me multiskilled?" "No," one of the trainers responded, "it would make you the manager."

In our workplaces we already have the preconditions for a multiskilled workforce. Our mobility and transfer provisions allow workers to apply for different jobs and there is a chance to develop skills that not only improve their jobs but improve production.

On the other hand multiskilling as I've described it using specific workplaces and actual jobs leads to:

1. decreased mobility rights (ie transfers, promotions),
2. an intensified work pace,
3. a general deterioration in the conditions of employment,
4. and fewer jobs.

This is what we call management by stress. Multiskilling can be the veneer that masks a new round of quicker, swifter, faster, which in turn translates into higher injuries and WCB (Workers Compensation Board) claims, higher absenteeism, poorer quality, a diminishing commitment to the production process and heightened levels of distrust in the workplace. All at a time when we need to move in the opposite direction.

Multiskilling The Trades

In the trades streams there are some new classifications, there are some overlapping responsibilities, but for the most part we are not talking about a new multi-trade or new combined trades. In fact, there is little evidence to suggest that a *multi-skilled craftworker* is emerging. And it is even rarer that multicrafting means acquiring certificates in more than one trade. Instead it means skilled trades workers who perform duties which are peripheral and incidental to their craft and it implies the development of a type of skilled trade generalist.

Both are problematic developments given the dramatic changes in the technical base of production. Look at our workplaces: the growth in the quantity of equipment, the greater variety in machinery, the increasing sophistication of each machine and the ongoing effort to network systems have made them more complex and complicated. But rather than updating and deepening the skills in our trades we are using valuable training time to superficially cross-train so that tradespeople can do the more general work common to all trades or the more incidental work unique to a particular trade.

What multiskilling offers is reportedly a solution to idle time, skilled trade labour costs and machine downtime. But under the cover of multiskilling are lurking a number of debates we should first resolve. One has to do with the *breadth* versus the *depth* of skills, and a related issue is the reference to *generalist* or *specialist*.

A number of months ago I was at a public meeting of the Ontario Premier's Council where a spokesperson for Toyota discussed his company's approach to training. The official talked about electricians and pointed out that his company needs only about 50 percent of what an electrician knows and suggested reforms in skilled trades training that would allow for a different type of electrician at Toyota. But what makes the electrician an electrician is that other 50 percent. The 50 percent that Toyota might not need is what provides skilled workers with a sense of competence and real mobility. But it is not only that; the other 50 percent allows electricians to make significant contributions to production.

I don't think filling up the electrician's time with other incidental tasks and duties is an effective substitute for deepening her or his skills. In fact we may be creating a future shortage of workers with in-depth skills.

There are some natural skill progressions we should be encouraging. Electricians learning more about electronics, machinists learning more about programming. I believe those developments are more valuable than millwrights taking quickie electrical courses or welders taking quickie courses in high pressure steam systems.

As a rule multiskilling proponents prefer generalists over specialists. But despite that preference I haven't yet heard of proposals to rotate designers with accountants, industrial engineers with corporate lawyers or for human resource managers to be cross-trained in marketing. Why should we accept it in the plant?

Toyota expects managers to be multifunctional. But think about the description of multifunctional managers. The overhead that was presented pointed out that "each manager must develop skills to be able to participate in a group decision."

But for Toyota's trades, multiskilling means something considerably different. As we were told the company is currently sending two tradesworkers to a problem area — a mechanical and an electrical one — but the intention is to be able in the future to send only one tradesworker. I will return to this point later.

Hybrid Skilled Worker

I have read about BMW in Munich and Alfa Romeo in Milan who have developed what has been called "hybrid skilled" workers in order to deal with the complex electro/mechanical problems inherent in the repair and maintenance of programmable automation.

BMW and Alpha Romeo chose the route of the "hybrid skilled worker." But other choices have been made to handle the repair and maintenance of programmable automation by swat teams or flying squads of highly trained specialists working effectively together. Both the hybrid skilled worker and the flying squad approach could effectively address the maintenance and repair requirements of the automation so the question is which is better — and that immediately raises other questions, such as better from whose perspective?

It is interesting how the concept of "hybrid skill" with its descriptive qualifiers such as broader, enlarged and more general, might in fact give way to more narrow and limited skills in the workplace and to a workforce which is less mobile, within the plant and within the economy.

We can agree that as a general trend workplaces are becoming more complex and individual machines are becoming more complicated. Given this trend it could be argued that instead of being more broadly capable in electro/mechanical repairs the "hybrid skills" worker is indeed the first step in a process of maintenance and repair becoming product, area or model specific. A skilled trade worker looks after the Toshiba CNCs and only the Toshiba CNCs, another is assigned to the Cinci gantry mills, some other "hybrid specialists" deal with the Mazaks lathes or the Ramboudi copy mills or the Kapp or the Gleasons or whatever. Indeed as the equipment becomes more sophisticated and intricate and correspondingly expensive, purchasers are demanding longer term service contracts with equipment suppliers. Depending on the extent and duration of these repair and maintenance contracts our production facilities could end up resembling the office where, for instance, when the photocopier is down Xerox or Canon or whoever is called in to repair it. Externalizing this set of skills to the supplier reinforces a dependency relationship and the in-plant contribution could end up being the equivalent of adding ink or paper to the photocopier. Once the complex set of electrical-electronic and mechanical skills are lost to a producing company the consequences for production are significant. What appears as a step forward could end up being two steps backward.

When it comes to maintenance, we are not simply talking about maximizing the rate of machine utilization. A 100 percent rate of operation could simply see us stockpiling production as inventory. Instead we are talking about operational availability which means the equipment operates when needed, it operates as long as it is needed and it operates with 100 percent satisfactory performance. In such a context maintenance means repairing and adjusting equipment so that it is always in its "optimum operating state." (This is a phrase I borrow from CAMI.)

In this approach the fact that some skilled trades are idle some of the time is not the issue. The issue is what is the best strategy for achieving the optimum operating state.

The maintenance strategy, I've been told, is always a trade-off between costs and benefits. Multiskilling, I think, confuses the short with the long-term.

There are two sets of figures to be concerned with. One, no doubt, is the percentage of lost production, due to waiting for the various trades to perform their respective roles. I know you all have at least one "waiting for maintenance" story. I'm sure you can all find some situation where you shake your heads in disbelief.

It could be an electrician waiting for a millwright to remove a metal guard in order to gain access to an electrical panel, or waiting for an electrician to disconnect a low-voltage cable so someone else can weld a broken bracket holding a motor, and so on.

But the second set of figures is the reduction in total lost production because of the quality of the skilled trade work performed. The first set of figures might move in one direction, the second set in a different direction.

The point is our cost/benefit analysis has to avoid the narrow economic calculus of labour costs or some superficial concept of reducing non-value added costs.

Let's get practical. The "waiting for maintenance" stories might tell us something should be done, but they don't supply the solution. They are not a substitute for analysis. Instead we need a clear assessment of the problems and a response to them.

It is ironic that in many of our workplaces our members are trained in analytic processes. They are taught the six steps of problem solving. There is training in using control charts and pareto diagrams, our members are encouraged to explore cause and effect relations, and to discover the root causes of problems by asking why five times.

Yet here we are with a solution — multiskilling — in search of a problem.

Solving Problems

Every union I know is willing to review and even revise work arrangements and practices. At times we even initiate the discussion. In the recent contract negotiations with the Big Three we argued for advance notice of technological change. One of the major reasons is so we can have enough time to assess the technology and to develop the appropriate training so our people can effectively work with the technology. For instance the skilled trades letter in Ford reads in part "seek to identify appropriate and specialized training so that employees will be capable of performing the new or changed work." That speaks to a willingness to change work practices.

The same can be said for cooperation. In small plants there

has always been an informal cooperation among the trades. It is a cooperation that works to the advantage of the skilled trades in those operations and to the advantage of management. It is not a case of skill dilution or work intensification. I think there is an opportunity to provide training that would allow our trades to more effectively work together. But that is different than multiskilling. It is more like how Toyota defines multiskilling among managers.

We will cooperate and we will try and solve problems. For example, a recent document signed with GM for a new Epoxy Die R and D facility reads in part:

> "The parties recognize that within the skilled trades classification there are certain skills and knowledge unique to individual trades. The parties also recognize that many skills are common among a variety of skilled trades classifications. Within the research and development project the process will necessitate a close working relationship between the trades involved. This will result in the need, within their skill and knowledge level, for employees of different trades to perform a wide variety of tasks."

It goes on to conclude:

> "Management assures the union that there is nc intent to adversely impact the integrity of individual skills trades classifications."

Here we have a situation which could work. The recognition of the integrity of the trades, the call for a close working relationship, the recognition of some natural overlap could evolve into a system of cooperation among specialists. Or management could focus on the phrase "performs a wide variety of tasks" and end up taking advantage of the situation. In other words the outcome could be beneficial or it could be detrimental depending on which sentiment defines the working relationships and work practices.

I started with a central principle that stated that a workplace should be an effective production system and at the same time an attractive place for human beings. I don't think that multiskilling moves us in that direction.

In terms of the safety of our workplaces, the uptime of the

equipment, the tolerances and quality of machine performance, the ability to contribute ideas to production, and the ability to work with new technology, our existing system (with some changes) is superior to the one proposed by the multiskilled version. And in terms of mobility and seniority rights and the confidence and skills of our members, there is no contest.

David Robertson is a national representative in the Research Department of CAW–Canada.

Chapter Four

Collective Bargaining And Training

Doug Olthius[1]

Let me begin with two questions. The first question is descriptive — and can be phrased in a number of ways: what has been, and is, the place of training in the collective bargaining process? How has training been bargained? How is training bargained now?

The second is a more forward-looking question: Where are we going? Is the role of training in the bargaining process likely to be much different in the future? Why and how might our traditional approaches to bargaining training be changing?

There are no single answers to these questions. But I hope to show what our experience has been with the Steelworkers. Keep in mind that we are a large, diverse private sector union. Our experience with these issues will be relevant for some unions but not others.

How Is Training Bargained?

As trade unionists, our involvement in bargaining training has always been tied to specific contexts. I see four general con-

---

1. The author wishes to acknowledge the work of Hugh Mackenzie, Research Director, United Steelworkers of America, which he used in the preparation of this paper.

texts around which our union bargains training:

1. *Access/rationing* of training opportunities. This type of bargaining would be related to job ladders or lines of progression, particularly in large industrial plants where workers need to be trained — usually on-the-job — to move up the line.
2. *Trades qualifications.* We bargain for apprenticeship programs, although with less and less success in recent years.
3. *Technological change.* We bargain for the right to be trained on new equipment, and we bargain for training for longer-service employees so they can bump into jobs that provide them the same standard of living.
4. *Lay-off.* I will come back to this case below.

In fact, there might be a fifth point to this list: in many workplaces we don't bargain training — however that might be defined — at all. Zero. None. Let me start with this last point.

As we discuss training and collective bargaining, we have to acknowledge — sometimes reluctantly — that the major force driving most collective bargaining is wages. Whatever other factors are at play, the central reality is that our members want and need money. If it isn't wages, it's pensions or benefits, paid wash-up time or paid lunches, twelve hour shifts or Sunday premiums. Sometimes it's health and safety, or job security, seniority and contracting out. Training is usually not even on the list; and if it is, it is normally not a major bargaining priority.

The neglect of training as a bargaining issue may be in part because of the way we have thought of training in the past. Training has always been something done by the employer. He or she makes all the decisions: the "what," "where," "why," even the "how" of training. Our only concern was with the "who": who gets it?

Of course, the training we got in this situation has always been whatever employers thought workers needed to do the job the way the employer had designed it. And, for the most part these needs have been defined in very specific terms: the need for skilled operators of complex new pieces of equipment; the need for highly specialized firm- or industry-specific skills such as steelmakers or rolling mill operators in the steel industry. The content of the training is determined by these specific needs. As a result, most traditional training is *task oriented* and directed toward a specific goal established by the employer.

The question of 'who' gets trained is where training and collective bargaining have traditionally met. *Collective bargaining related to training, where it exists, has traditionally been oriented toward the rationing of these very specific employer-determined opportunities.* It has generally not addressed at all the broader questions of the type of training being offered or any relationship to the needs of the worker/trainees.

But now, to return to the fourth point above, there is one major exception to what I have been saying. That is the situation of lay-off or plant closure, which we call adjustment training. In these situations, there is normally no specific context for training, so the training offered is generally directed towards the individual needs and wants rather than the needs of any specific employer. While much of this type of training is directed towards enhancing "employability" and therefore constrained by employer needs in a general sense, by its very nature it must be driven by the perceived needs of the individual.

Unfortunately, our union has had a great deal of experience with training in the context of layoffs or shutdowns. One of the things that is noteworthy about this experience is the astonishing variety of training activity that takes place in these situations. Groups of people who would have been exposed to a very narrow range of training programs and opportunities while working at the plant will often take advantage of a much broader range of activities when they are no longer constrained by the needs of their particular employer. While a lot of this variety is forced by the need to find new employment, it also suggests that there are significant training possibilities that are not addressed by the traditional approach.

Where Do We Go Now?

This brings me to the second question I set out at the start: where now? Is there any reason to believe that collective bargaining related to training will change? Many union activists certainly would like it to change. We are agreed that "more training" is not enough. We want to move beyond the "who" of training, although that is clearly important, to the "what" of training. The content. We reject employer-based competency training; we want to insist on worker-based developmental training.

But one note of caution here. In our discussions around this issue I think we must be careful not to suggest that job or firm-specific skills are unimportant. On the contrary. Workers have a clear interest in such skills. In some sense it really is "our" knowledge, and it is passed on between workers themselves. Workers' understanding and knowledge of the way their jobs work is often far more advanced and thorough than their bosses' knowledge. It is this informal knowledge and skill, and the willingness of workers to share it and apply it, that can make all the difference between a dynamic and efficient production process and an inefficient process. As employers have discovered, workers' informal skills can be the basis of major productivity increases. *They also often form one of the major bases of union bargaining strength.*

Our training agenda, therefore, should seek balance. Our training goal must be to complement workers' tacit knowledge — their shop-floor understanding developed through years of experience — with a much greater commitment to formal training in broad principles: generic or developmental training.

So maybe we should ask ourselves, how likely are we to make headway in this area through collective bargaining? Or is collective bargaining not the appropriate place to fight these battles at all?

Our success in bargaining will depend on at least two things. On the one hand, it will depend in large part on how badly our members feel the need for a new approach to training opportunities. On the other, it will depend upon how hard employers resist. Is it possible for management to find something in worker-centred training that they can use as well?

Union members have complained about the inadequacies of training for many years. Those complaints have never translated into bargaining issues. Are there workplace pressures now which will change all that? Perhaps so. You might sum them up as increased job insecurity. This is important because as long as we think our jobs are safe, many of us don't think twice about training. We don't have much of a problem with employer-driven training that is job or firm specific, provided of course that we have some say in who gets the training.

But the 1980s has been a world of transitory firms and industries undergoing virtually constant structural and technological change. The 1990s look much the same. The traditional model of a lifetime job with a single employer has become the exception rather than the rule.

In my union's major bargaining units such as Stelco, Algoma and Inco, there hasn't been an appreciable amount of hiring in nearly 15 years. Thousands were laid off in the early 1980s; thousands more took early retirement and were not replaced. The big, stable employers of the 1970s are no longer as big or as stable as they were, and they are no longer a significant source of new employment. The implications of this kind of change for the training system are profound.

First, the more rapid turnover of firms and of employees in firms makes it even more likely that employers will avoid training obligations for everyone except possibly a core group of highly valued employees. Widely available training is, from the firm's point of view simply going to be wasted — or even worse — is going to benefit other firms.

Second, the steady decline in the proportion of the workforce that is so-called lifetime employment means that firm-specific training is steadily declining in value both for society as a whole and for the individuals concerned. Training whose application is limited to particular workplaces, firms or industries, no longer meets the needs of workers.

Third, the pace of technological and structural change in the economy means that in the future our members may be concerned more about opportunities to train for new jobs than about the relative pay and other rights associated with the job they currently have. That is speculative. The point is that today there may in fact be workplace-based pressures to begin to bargain training in a different way than we traditionally have. Perhaps we should ask a more fundamental question: is there a collective right to training? Or, more perhaps more appropriately, can we build that right through collective bargaining?

Training As A Collective Right

The opportunities for negotiating training-content and worker-oriented training on a plant- or firm-specific basis are rather limited. The largest firms employing thousands of workers may be the exception. But operating on their own narrow profit motive, even big firms won't likely become major trainers. It simply is not in the individual employer's interest to invest in training to the extent that society requires and in the form that will be of greatest benefit to the individual worker. The employer will always tend to under-invest, and to support only training that is directly linked to his or her short-term economic interests.

So new institutional arrangements are going to be required to ensure both that adequate levels of training investment are made and that those investments are more responsive to the needs of workers as distinct from the needs of the firm. And new arrangements will require new and different resources of several kinds.

First, better training arrangements and more of them will require more money. That may or may not be forthcoming from the governments of the day. But beyond that — union involvement is also critical. Without trade union involvement, commitments of additional public resources to training are little more than an invitation to the larger more sophisticated employers to raid the public treasury. A classic case in point is the major share of federal training funds taken by banks and other large financial institutions. In those cases, we know that it is mostly management who gets the training.

The reality is that an individual right to training cannot be realized if it is not asserted. And only the trade union movement is in a position to articulate that right and to create the institutional framework within which it can flourish.

There are a number of experiments underway in worker

involvement in training and adjustment. These include the Sectoral Skills Council in the Electrical and Electronics Equipment Manufacturers' Association of Canada (EEMAC), the Canadian Steel Trade and Employment (CSTEC), and the Automotive Parts Sectoral Training Council (APSTC). These initiatives challenge our organizations to find new ways to address membership concerns about training. They push us far beyond the traditional union role of rationalizing and organizing access to whatever the employer wants to offer. They put training on the agenda of labour relations. As unionists, we are just learning how to work in these arrangements and how to make them responsive to our demands.

In sum, I have no doubt "training" will become a more important bargaining objective. But, I don't believe that will take place, *in the first instance*, within firm- or plant-specific bargaining. Instead, I think the "what," "why," and "how" of training can be more easily addressed via new institutional arrangements, using public dollars to give us critical leverage. Management wants public training dollars. That gives us an edge in the process of social bargaining. Once those arrangements are in place, individual negotiating committees at the traditional bargaining table may be able to bargain training more effectively.

Doug Olthius is a Research Associate in the National Office of United Steelworkers of America.

Chapter Five

Fighting for Training: Fighting for a Future
André Beckerman

Why did Wayne Clayton lose his job?

In a recent issue of the *Globe & Mail's* glossy *Report on Business Magazine*, an article called "The Human Scrap Heap" claimed: "For Wayne Clayton and 137,000 other recent blue-collar layoffs, the real enemy is not the current recession, it's their lack of job skills."

Well, that is bullshit! The real enemy, I agree, is not "the recession," but neither is it lack of job skills. The real enemy is the Mulroney federal government. This is the government that reacted to a downturn in the business cycle with high interest rates, a high dollar and free trade — first with the U.S.A. and now with Mexico as well. This is the government that has privatized key parts of our national infrastructure, like Air Canada and Petro-Canada, cut back on Via Rail and continues to drastically underfund still other crucial national institutions like the CBC. Each of these policies has caused direct job losses by the thousands, as well as further indirect job losses in the companies which supplied and serviced the first group.

The real enemy? It's also the multinational (mainly American-based) and the Canadian-based corporations that use the downturn in the economy as an opportunity to withdraw their capital from established industries. Then they either reinvest abroad or re-deploy their capital in sectors that produce good capital gains but accelerate the cycle of job loss and deindustrialization.

The outcome of these policies is sustained double-digit unemployment rates in Ontario and rates over 16 percent in such heavily industrialized communities as Windsor. The so-called "current recession" has come to look and feel more like a depression.

Why worry about training — isn't the government "doing it?" What is the relevance of an issue like training in this increasingly disastrous economy? The 1990 Premier's Council report of the Ontario Liberal government of David Peterson, *People and Skills in the New Global Economy*, identified industrial training as a key strategy if Ontario was to compete successfully in the world economy. Yet, that same government, through its Ministry of Skills Development, had in 1989–90 committed $33.7 million to corporation-directed training and a grand $4 million to self-directed retraining programs for workers. That was before the roof fell in, both for the economy and, thankfully, for that government. The Premier's Council report stated:

> "The 1987 Statistics Canada survey ... reported that less than one quarter of firms in Canada spend money on training their employees. Studies conducted for the Ontario Ministry of Skills Development reinforce this finding ... The evidence collected by the Ministry further indicates that training tends to be piecemeal, uncoordinated and poorly planned, even among those firms which do provide it. Moreover, the report of the Federal Government's Advisory Council on Adjustment indicates that in those firms which do offer training, it is directed disproportionately to employees who already have above-average education and pay" (1990, p. 92).

In addition, since 1985, the federal government has been systematically reducing the transfer payments to provinces for training in public sector institutions like community colleges. It has been redirecting these funds instead to corporations and to private-sector training agencies — the familiar "terrible twins" of privatization and contracting out. The consequences of these policies are loss of quality in the training offered and the skimming off of profit from already reduced funds for training activity. Judging by this track record, training cannot safely be left to a Tory federal government, nor to Liberal or Tory provincial governments. Why worry about training when the economy is collapsing around us? I see a number of compelling reasons:

1. Capital is redeploying its resources out of many areas of industrial activity. Most of the jobs lost will not be regained later in a period of growth.
2. The areas of the economy that are attracting capital and that will be the mainstays of a renewed economy are less labour-intensive than the sectors that are currently shutting down or reducing production and employment.
3. The enterprises that will continue to operate and will rebound as part of an economic recovery will operate at a higher technological level and will be less labour-intensive than they were before the economic crash. Employers do now, and will increasingly, invest in new technology and in training of a greatly reduced workforce to make this possible.

The Future: A Massive Human Scrap Heap?

This all adds up to a massive "human scrap heap." It's a vision of hell for at least 10 percent, perhaps as much as 20 percent of Canadian workers who still expect to make a living in a "normal" economy, if they can somehow survive the recession. The futility of this hope is only too visible south of the border, where the U.S. seems quite willing to allow its workforce to split into two parts. One part consists of a diminishing employed "elite" of relatively well-educated and technologically well-trained workers who will continue to enjoy an affluent lifestyle. The other consists of a rapidly growing underclass of less educated, less skilled workers who depend on minimum waged, unskilled, insecure and dead-end "McJobs." This second group is only one small step away from those who have no work at all, nor any prospects of employment, and have become terminally trapped in poverty and dependence on welfare programs. Together, they are a rapidly-growing underclass of millions of people.

Can Canada Resist The Trend?

In Canada, the battle is not yet lost; in fact, it has only begun. In contrast to the U.S. where the labour movement has almost ceased to be a major force, our union movement is still growing and vigorous. While the Mulroney government and its various provincial collaborators continue to ravage our economy, the election of the NDP in Ontario, B.C. and Saskatchewan, and the strength of the NDP support federally still hold out hopes for a much needed change in key economic policies.

Avoiding the nightmarish future can only be achieved by a combination of drastic reversal of government policy combined with strong counter-measures by the labour movement. Canadian society can save itself by relying on our distinctive institutions: a vigorous social-democratic tradition that has significant enough support to be able to form the government in key provinces and a labour movement committed to social unionism.

Fighting for training should be seen as an important part of this fight to preserve a decent future for the Canadian working class as a whole.

Training: who decides and who gets trained?

Unfortunately, increased emphasis on training, in itself, does not prevent the "human scrap heap" of the immediate future. It depends on who gets trained and how. It's true that corporations, especially the larger ones, are increasing their training activity — but often at public expense. And workers who are offered company-controlled training are understandably eager to take advantage of it, since it enhances their employment security and earnings. But this is not always good news.

The problem is that most corporation-initiated training is narrow, directed to corporate needs in the short term. It does little to equip a worker for longer-term flexibility or the ability to keep up with technological change. Even worse, training is mainly offered to the best-educated, best-trained minority. The reason is obvious enough — a well-trained worker can be "trained up" to a further level of competence more quickly and more cheaply than a worker starting from a lower skill or education level. There is also such a thing as being "trained oriented." A person who has already taken training will more confidently and easily take further training.

As long as training decisions are controlled by the corporations, the danger is real of creating a division of the working class into a highly trained elite and a marginally employed or increasingly unemployed and unemployable "underclass." It is a frightening possibility.

Union Principles About Training:

The Ontario Federation of Labour adopted, at its 1989 Convention, a position paper on training [see Appendix I] including several key principles. I would state the principles this way:

Democracy	Training should be a right much as public education to Grade 12 is currently recognized as a right.
Accountability	Training should be publicly administered and delivered by public educational institutions.
Control & Funding	Training should be largely publicly funded and publicly controlled, enhancing accountability and democracy by making it generally available.
Content of Training	Training should be broad-based, designed to enhance the academic as well as technical knowledge, skill and ability of those taking training programs. The objective should be to enhance broad technological literacy so working people are able to progress with increasingly complex technological development over the period of a working life. The concept of "lifelong learning" is tied to this goal.

Private Training	Training done by private employers should be funded by employers themselves as is done in many other countries. The nature and delivery of such training should be decided jointly with the union representing the affected workers.

Acting On Our Principles:
Political Action & Collective Bargaining

To give life to these principles requires two forms of action. One is to step up organized political pressure on those governments that can be influenced, and to redouble our efforts to replace those that cannot. Where it is possible to elect NDP governments, developing a progressive training policy is then achievable if the labour movement works with progressive educators and builds public support. Ontario NDP Premier Bob Rae is quoted as saying, "The old concept of education beginning in kindergarten and finishing in high school or university has died. The challenge for teachers and the government now is to come up with 'creative' ways to retain those who have left the school system" (*Globe & Mail*, April 8, 1991).

The other type of action is our traditional one: using collective bargaining to achieve our goals. The existing needs of our members and the initiatives of the employers have made training an issue in the workplace for a long time and our unions have made some progress on these issues, but we need to escalate the fight.

First, a few general observations:

1. Progress in winning "training rights" in collective agreements is very uneven. Unions negotiating with heavy industry — CAW and Steelworkers — have achieved some rights, as have the Postal Workers. Few others have been able to gain significant rights.

2. The "training rights" negotiated have usually been won in contracts with the largest corporations. Even unions that have done well in their main contracts have not had the

same ability to negotiate in contracts with middle-sized or small employers.
3. Some unions have taken the strategy of providing the training themselves, funding it by a combination of government grants, contributions negotiated with a group of employers and members' dues money.
4. In most collective agreements, training is treated as an issue of individual mobility and/or job security. It is rare to achieve it as a collective right.

These observations serve to highlight the fact that negotiating training issues is very difficult. In many industries, employers have been able to retain almost total control of who gets trained, in what way and over the content of the training.

Contract Clauses On Training — Description & Some Current Experience

Job Postings: Of the collective agreement clauses that touch on the issue of training, the most common is on job posting. The issue arises on the requirement that among qualified applicants for a posted job, the successful candidate must be "able to perform" the vacant job. Where employers used this provision to avoid accepting a senior and qualified applicant in favour of someone they preferred, they claimed that "ability to perform" meant performing the whole job with no preparation. Since that is often impossible without at least some "training," employers used this to get around the issue of seniority and maintain control of job postings. Unions often respond by negotiating a "familiarization" or "training" period which forces the employer to allow a worker a fair chance at a new job and reinforces the principle of filling vacancies by seniority.

Layoff & Bumping: The same issue comes up in layoffs: in order to "bump" by seniority, contract language usually demands that a worker be able to perform the job of a junior employee being "bumped." Employers use this replacement to protect junior employees they may prefer as against a more senior employee facing layoff who may be a union activist or not docile enough in his or her attitude to the employer. The same type of protection is then demanded by the union: a "familiarization" or short "training period."

Dealing With Individual Rights: These two problems, advancement and layoffs, are faced in every workplace and are usually negotiated early on in the bargaining relationship. By tying job security to length of service, a worker's right to advance from job to job and the right to use seniority to avoid layoff, are taken out of the employer's "discretion" and become rights that can be enforced.

Even so, they are limited since they don't contest the employer's ability to control training and impose technology on the workforce itself. This allows the employer control of technological competence to control the people who make up the workforce.

"Tuition Support" For Adult Education: Many contracts provide that an employer will refund the tuition for work-related courses that an employee might take on his or her own time. Some of the contract clauses go a bit further, providing time off to write exams or limited allowance for expenses.

The striking thing is that in job-related courses taken by a worker on his/her own time, the worker is taking the initiative and contributing time, effort and some money to get the training that the employer should be providing on paid working time. In return, providing the worker gets permission in advance and succeeds in the course, he/she may get a refund of tuition. What a sweet deal! The employer gets a more qualified worker, with the cost shared between the worker and the taxpayers who provide the training — at virtually no cost to the employer.

Where a union has pushed further, or where the employer is more progressive, the same right may exist for non-job-related courses. But again, the worker has to bear almost the whole cost in time, effort and money to act on the concept of "lifelong learning."

In my experience, it is rare to see a collective agreement that provides paid time off for a course that a worker decides to take. By contrast, paid time is quite normal on employer-directed training courses, with or without language in the collective agreement.

Obviously, a central issue in these provisions is control — employers want the right to decide about training. Another is cost — employers want a free ride with the worker and the taxpayer carrying the burden. A third is that these types of provisions in a contract only address individual situations and don't deal with the greater issue of training for the workforce as a whole.

Union Participation In Training

In more up-to-date workplaces, especially since the "Human Resource Department" replaced the good old "Personnel Department," it is increasingly common to have "Human Resource Strategies" printed on glossy paper stuffed into pay envelopes.

It is in these more "modern" corporations that unions have won the right to participate in training committees, either by bargaining for it or, in some cases, by invitation. The problem is a familiar one: is the union present on the committee as window dressing to make the company-controlled program look more legitimate, or even to satisfy public funding policies that require employee representation? Or do the worker representatives have genuine power to veto inappropriate programs, negotiate wage support for hours spent in training and ensure the training is going to benefit the workers over the long term?

These are difficult issues. It is nonsense to demand a simon-pure approach and refuse to participate unless all desirable criteria are met. Our members would feel ill-served if we took the position of abstaining from any role that is not perfect in every way.

It is exactly in dealing with these complexities that we must use the full range of weapons at our disposal: hard bargaining in formal negotiations for the collective agreement to nail down the strongest possible rights in training committees and tough persistent infighting at the workplace to insist that representatives on training committees have real power and are not acting as window-dressing.

Boycotting a committee, or boycotting the training itself is a valid tactic, providing the members are united and clear on the objective and will stand together — sometimes for a lengthy period of time.

Another difficult issue is where quite valid and well-designed training policies are negotiated at an industry or corporation-wide level, but don't have workplace-oriented implementation systems. In those cases, a good program, designed and negotiated at the top, can be inflexible, authoritarian and self-defeating when it comes down to the level of the work groups and individuals.

Some Recent Experiences In The Ontario Public Service Employees Union (OPSEU)

To bring some of these problems closer to home, and especially to encourage those who may feel that the difficulties are overwhelming, I want to offer a couple of examples of training issues that my union has been pursuing, and where we feel we are making progress. These are not cited in order to blow our own horn — many unions are taking strong initiatives with equal or greater success, so I am outlining these particular cases as examples I happen to be involved in directly.

The Public Service

OPSEU represents over 55,000 workers employed directly by the Province of Ontario in the Public Service. For that portion of our membership, the overwhelming problem is legislation: the Crown Employees Collective Bargaining Act (CECBA) expressly reserves all issues of training to the exclusive jurisdiction of the Crown — the employer. Over the years, the union has challenged this, as well as other restrictive parts of the legislation, at the Public Service Labour Relations Tribunal. The tribunal has consistently upheld the restrictions and prevented the union from pursuing training at the formal negotiating table.

Yet, reality has made it impossible to leave training in the hands of the top public service bureaucrats. In the case of the provincial jail system, in psychiatric hospitals and in treatment centres for the developmentally handicapped, it is a matter of life and death for our members. Assaults by prisoners or clients on each other and on the staff are a constant and long-term reality. Insufficient staffing and use of untrained staff directly threatens the inmates, patients and the staff. Illegal direct work actions by the staff, especially in the jails, have forced some negotiations on training issues despite the law. In the case of ambulance officers employed by the Ministry of Health, training issues are under active negotiations, despite the legal restrictions. In these areas, our motivation for forcing the issue, despite the law, is the horrendous record of injuries and death — three ambulance officers killed in the line of duty in the last two years, for reasons that the union alleges include inadequate training systems put in place by the employer.

The progress we are able to make in working around the law is not enough — a major issue under discussion between OPSEU and the Rae government is a thorough reform of the Crown Employees Collective Bargaining Act, including removing its many limits on free collective bargaining. The discussion is proceeding and we fully expect a remedy in the coming months. The effect of such reform will not only benefit our members in the public service but will also set the tone for an opening up of training as a democratic right of workers in the province generally.

Ambulance Services

In an ambulance service in Hamilton represented by our union which, until recently, was one of the dozens of contracted-out, privately-owned (but publicly-funded) services, our members were given the opportunity to train to become "paramedics" — that is, to take specialized training beyond basic life support skills that all ambulance officers are required to have. For the members, as skilled and dedicated professionals, it was an attractive idea. Then came the conditions: the program was designed by the bureaucrats in the Ministry of Health, would be delivered by a hospital and administered by the company that "owned" the ambulance service. There would be no significant input by the ambulance officers or their union on the content, selection, timing, eligibility or costs of training, the wage premium for the additional skills nor any negotiations on the rules under which the new skills would be exercised — nor on the liabilities and penalties that could potentially result in lawsuits or discharge when the worker exercised their expanded skills.

The quandary was not unusual: the workers were told that if they didn't volunteer, others would and they would be left behind. The usual implication that failure to volunteer would not look good on their work record was also there.

Faced with this difficult choice, the twelve ambulance officers involved decided to resist — they stood together and refused to take the program. Subtle and not-so-subtle threats and pressures only succeeded in persuading two of the group to go ahead — the rest stood firm. After a standoff that lasted over a year, an accommodation was reached. Some of the workers' concerns were met and they agreed to take the program and a "paramedic" system was put in place. The same issue was fought out in several other ambulance services in the province with mixed results.

As a result of a long campaign by ambulance workers and the three unions who represent them — OPSEU, CUPE and the SEIU — a government inquiry into ambulance service in the province of Ontario is just beginning. Training is one of the issues highlighted by the unions and we hope to be able to force a training policy that will recognize ambulance workers' needs and rights and permit them to provide the first-class service to the people of the province that has been unavailable because of policies of privatization, bureaucratic control and stifling of the professionalism and dedication of the ambulance workers. Again, training is a vital issue — for self-preservation of the workers as well as for the sake of the public who depend on ambulance services. It is too vital to be left to the bosses.

Ryerson

A few years ago, our union was negotiating a first collective agreement for the 500 support staff of Ryerson Polytechnical Institute. The group included a broad range of office and administrative workers and many people exercising very specialized technical skills. As bargaining went on over several months, we experienced the usual difficulties over seniority rights, classifications and wages. One group of workers in the bargaining unit was the cafeteria operation, staffed largely by middle-aged immigrant women workers. As bargaining went on, rumours of a management decision to contract out the cafeteria became more persistent. We found that a straight "no contracting out" clause was not achievable and raised the demand for retraining as part of a guarantee of continued employment if that operation, or any other, was to be contracted out.

The employer, an educational institution, reacted very strongly — they had been somewhat willing to agree to general technological upgrading provisions in the contract, but here they drew the line. They ridiculed our position, arguing that taking middle-aged immigrant women workers with a low educational level and limited job skills and guaranteeing them employment in a high-skilled, technologically advanced environment was unreasonable.

We took the issue to the membership meeting where the strike vote was held. We asked the workforce to take a stand, exactly on the principle — were these workers to be scrapped, sacrificed to the cost-savings of contracting out or was this the time to stand and fight?

Although the workforce had been only partially supportive of the union until then, the strike vote was 90 percent. The vast majority of the Ryerson workers saw this as an issue of equity — that workers had a right to be trained to be able to continue to earn a living, even where, or especially where, it would require considerable academic upgrading as well as technological training.

A short strike helped solve the remaining issues and the principle was won — not in all the details that might have been required, but the workers had enforced a principle, that equity is an important issue in training.

Ontario Community Colleges

OPSEU represents the 9,500 faculty and nearly 6,000 support staff in the twenty-three community colleges in the province. Thousands of part-time support workers and part-time and sessional faculty are prevented by legislation from being represented by the union, another item of overdue legislative reform that OPSEU is pressing the NDP government to clean up.

The colleges are seen by many, including the labour movement, as the prime agency of training and retraining in the province and this was one of their prime functions from their inception. Ironically, in their relationship with their own employees, the colleges have illustrated nearly all the problems faced by workers in trying to win training rights from employers. Over the years, thousands of support staff jobs have been contracted out to avoid paying union rates. Cleaning, security, cafeteria, parking and other services in many of the colleges are performed by low-paid employees of private contractors, with few benefits, if any, no job security and access to none of the advantages of working for a public educational institution.

Throughout the decade of the 1980s, consistent underfunding and governance problems in the colleges produced increasing cutbacks in courses and progressive job insecurity for college employees. In the fall of 1989, bargaining for the province-wide agreements for support staff and faculty came to a crisis point. The support group had stressed retraining and an end to contracting out as part of its job security demands. Faculty had focused on retraining to prevent job loss. Both groups held province-wide strike votes in September/October 1989. The support staff won the vote by the narrowest of margins and negotiated a settlement which included a thorough joint study of contracting out, with a view to negotiating a solution at the next negotiations, and some improvements in job security, including some gains on the principle of retraining.

A faculty strike was called with a narrow majority vote. It lasted four weeks and ended with an agreement to arbitrate the issues. The result of the negotiations and strike were largely on the issues of retraining as it relates to job security along with resolution of a long-standing issue about vesting of sick leave accumulation.

Layoff provisions, which are heavily process-oriented, were cleaned up to strengthen the right to retain employment based on seniority. Where colleges had been able to layoff full-time faculty while parcelling the work out to non-union (and far lower-paid) sessional and part-time teachers, new provisions for the first time gave the teacher facing layoff the right to such work assignments in order to remain employed.

One of the most painfully won, and then only partially won, rights was retraining itself. Even after a month of strike, a period of paid retraining was provided for three months and only after all other alternatives were used. The guarantee of continued employment following the retraining is somewhat ambiguous. A more grudging and tight-fisted approach would be hard to devise — except for one with no rights at all, which had been the case previously.

Another new provision of the faculty agreement, and one which is probably even more significant, is the "Employment Stability Committee." A step forward from existing and relatively limited "joint consultation" committees, the "employment stability" approach has a specific mandate to analyze trends within the college in advance, in order to identify job instability before it impacts. Its duty is then to devise strategies to cope with the problem.

The solutions this committee can recommend to the college administration are very wide-ranging, including re-deployment of staff, re-organization of the work, use of existing mechanisms like sabbaticals and also retraining. If it were confined to acting as yet another consultative group, it would be of limited interest. What gives this new structure much more importance is that it is at least partially set up on a co-determination model. Its membership is equal, with representatives of the college administration and local union. It has freedom to gather data and agree on recommendations to the college, but more importantly, a levy of $50 per faculty member per year is put into a special fund controlled by the committee. The committee has the right to fully control use of these funds to implement its job stability strategy and a special fast arbitration system is in place to resolve disagreements within the committee. Beyond the special fund itself, the college may be asked to provide further funds, and must continue to fund its responsibilities under other job security provisions of the contract, including the guaranteed retraining clause. Many leaders of our faculty local unions see a lot of potential in this new type of committee, precisely because it has given the union real control over at least part of the staffing and retraining process.

Solutions On Training: A Blueprint?

The analysis and examples given surely illustrate the point that there is no single blueprint for action. While many believe that the government in its role as employer should set the standard by acting as a model employer, the reality is that we are still fighting just for the right to negotiate training issues. Free collective bargaining on training issues is not yet legally possible.

Where vital public interest and life and safety of both citizens and public employees are at stake, in the jails, in psychiatric hospitals, in facilities for the developmentally handicapped, technically illegal action by OPSEU members has forced a small beginning.

In the ambulance field, our members had to die on the job before some recognition of training issues as legitimate subjects of concern could start.

In institutions dedicated to training as their reason for existence, Ryerson and the community colleges, strong consistent action, including strikes by the employees, were required before any progress could be achieved. Even there, the fight is far from over.

Taking these examples from the experience of my union, hard, bold struggle in collective bargaining, backed up by strikes, is mandatory if we are to get anywhere.

The other half of the solution must also be pushed: unless governments can be persuaded to remove the obstacles of reactionary legislation, repressive policies and underfunding, our struggle on the collective bargaining front will produce small steps forward at enormous cost in struggle by our members.

If we are to avoid the horrendous future that can be seen south of the border, our government institutions must cease being part of the problem — they have to work with the union movement to begin work on the solutions.

André Beckerman is senior negotiator for the Ontario Public Service Employees Union (OPSEU).

Chapter Six

Unions And Training In Ontario
D'Arcy Martin

Common Sense And Good Sense

My work is training. For more than 12 years, I've trained union members how to stand up for their rights — on the job, in the union and in society. In the past few years, my role has focused especially on training policy development, supporting the union leaders in the Ontario Premier's Council and negotiating terms of union participation in the Sectoral Skills Council in the electrical and electronic manufacturing industry. From all of these experiences, I have learned a lot about training and about social bargaining over training. I am very enthusiastic about both. I think training has the potential today that health and safety had a decade ago — to engage a whole new group of members in union life, and to broaden union advocacy. But that will only happen if we choose our actions wisely. While staffers and national leaders have a contribution to make in setting union policy directions on training, we also need to consider ways of weaving in the voices of local union members.

Street-smart unionists can hear the difference between being talked at and talked with. We can smell a rat when those who wield power over us talk about "empowerment." And we know that, unless we intervene radically in education and training, as in the economy, "them what has most gets most." These and other lessons from union education can help us when we address provincial policy on training.

So let me start off with five basic propositions about training that seem common sense. We need to probe them, to distill the good sense that lies within each one.

The Status Quo On Training Isn't Acceptable

Sometimes we get mad, and want to pack the whole thing in. It's normal in union life to get frustrated by the scale of what's needed and the limited resources at hand to build it. This can happen with grievances, with safety and health, with pay equity and so on.

In regard to training, we just can't afford to take the attitude "it's my way or the highway." In the information age, workers' access to educational capital is decisively important, both individually and collectively. Dropping training from our bargaining agenda today is tantamount to dropping wages from negotiations just because we don't like the wage offer. We may argue about priorities, and may strike and boycott along the way, but we have to move the line forward on training. Because the status quo just isn't acceptable.

Training Matters In Terms Of Union Presence In The Workplace

Training could increase our relevance to our members, or it could de-fang us. In the past, our daily union activities have mostly touched the minority of workers who have personal disputes with management. Now, through health and safety, union counselling and other initiatives, we are gradually knitting unionism into the lives of the 3/4 of our members who ignore the union between rounds of bargaining.

Current union education touches 3 to 5 percent a year of our members, for relatively short periods of time. To get a voice in the ongoing battle for hearts and minds, we need to move out of this corner, into the centre of the ring. Input into job training provides this important possibility.

Training Isn't Good Or Bad In Itself

I used to think some training was better than no training. Now I'm not so sure. The work of Nancy Jackson and others has shown us how "competency-based training" can undermine the working knowledge already in the hands of workers. So maybe not all training is good for us.

But also, there's a difference between what is taught and what is learned. Those of us who work as educators know that deeply. Workers are ingenious about taking some control over production systems designed to be top-down. In the same way, there's something about adult learning that is particularly difficult to control. Once a worker has the time to reflect on his or her job, and to develop a new skill of any sort, it's hard for anyone to steer that person in predictable ways. That's why I think its important to get our members involved in training programs early, and not wait until they are sanitized to our satisfaction before our members can have access to them.

Job Training Has Been Put On The Table By Management, Not By Us

Employers need more training for their own reasons, and are inclined in most cases to run it under the "management rights" clause. Every unionist in Canada has agreed to this clause as part of each collective agreement, and few of us have negotiated training provisions that substantially reduce management's discretionary authority over access, content and method of training skills. So employers still largely control the agenda.

Contrast this with health and safety training, which was driven from the grass roots. In Ontario, union leaders have been playing catch-up to the members ever since miners walked off the job over health issues in the 1970s. The determination of members has got us to where we are today. Job training doesn't have this kind of history. It hasn't boiled up from the members as a union issue, and until member voices balance the discourse of the technocrats, we will all be vulnerable to manipulation.

*Training Is Being Proposed,
Not Just As A Workplace Activity But As Part
Of A Broader Social Contract With The Employers*

Part of the reason training is so controversial within the labour movement is that it is a cipher for the battle over a social contract. Important issues can get lost in the shuffle, like Third World countries in the old East-West polarization.

What the employers want out of training is flexibility to reorganize work and skills in order to boost productivity. What we want out of training is security and dignity on the job, with choices about life-long learning in the hands of the workers. The time and place for these disparate agendas to be negotiated is not agreed upon, nor are the mechanisms for accountability in place. So what do we do? Do we wait for a broader social contract to be in place before moving on training? Or do we wade in and use the process to move us closer to the broad social contract we desire? Training is a new arena of challenge; let's not sabotage it before it even gets off the ground.

From Side Track To Express Lane

In the past few years, my work on training has been steered from a side track to an express lane. In February 1990, the OFL (Onterio Federation of Labour) asked me to do a short presentation to a committee of the Premier's Council. They wanted a labour presentation to balance some corporate types who were coming in to sell "innovative" ideas on training. The invitation was based on the fact that I had done some work years before on the federal policy process called "Learning a Living." For most unionists, training policy has been hit-and-miss in this way. It has been on a side track. Every once in a while somebody calls us to rush out and present "the labour view" to some authority. But normal life was responding to local union requests for courses.

The question this points to is: who handles training in the unions? In the central labour bodies it is not entirely clear. Sometimes it's the education staff, sometimes it's the research staff. In affiliates the same is the case. Sometimes it's the education people, sometimes it's research, sometimes it's people who are actually servicing reps. Within locals the same is the case.

This chaotic picture points to a larger problem, that of overextension. If unions are going to take on a growing commitment to training, we need resources to do so, resources that are not stolen from other urgent work. What's happening now is that the people who are most interested in it are grabbing it. That includes me. I'm grabbing it. I think it matters. But this isn't systematic, to put it mildly.

Take, for instance, the way I got called in 1990 to do a labour presentation. It's typical of the way that we have handled training in the past, on the side track. The president of my union, Fred Pomeroy, sits on the Ontario Premier's Council. One December night in 1989, he had insomnia so he stayed up and read all the documents for a Premier's Council meeting the next day on training. I don't know who strengthened his coffee that previous evening, but certainly Ontario workers owe a debt to whomever did it, because he arrived on the morning plane from Ottawa absolutely ranting. He went into the Premier's Council, dominated by corporate and government people and said "this stuff is totally unacceptable, either it changes or we are walking out." He knew that the draft was technocratic, reactionary and elitist. To his shock and horror, Premier Peterson snapped back, "If you're so smart, why don't you write it? We will fund you to rewrite the report."

Fred Pomeroy walked over to the union office and said to me: "Look, I don't want you to misunderstand, I think you should have Christmas Day off." I appreciated his balance, but clearly I couldn't do it alone. So I looked around. There were three of us from the labour movement positioned to do this work because we occasionally backed up one of the three labour ranking officers on this training side track. So we still had to reach out to our allies. We assembled a think tank to work with the labour movement on this policy issue, because we couldn't keep up with the speed and intricacy of changes on our own.

In this case, I went particularly to the people around *Our Schools/Our Selves*, David Clandfield and others, and they gave extremely important support. Let's bear in mind that when we do that as a trade union movement as in all coalitions, we don't just always get our way. Sometimes David Clandfield's views made me nervous, and I'd say "I don't know how the labour movement is going to react to that." He would respond, "Well come on, you've got to bend too." So there is a process of social negotiation that goes on with our allies. We've got to be open to that.

With great effort, we produced a counter report. It was gorgeous. We thought maybe business would walk away from the table. Then we would print our version, a nice clean counter report, and get out with our hands clean. Instead, the business representatives said, "Okay, we'll bargain." We went into a process of social bargaining that lasted for three or four months. Line by line.

The union side was coordinated by John O'Grady of the OFL, very very skillfully. But the process was closed to other participants. There were a number of people who had a stake in that debate, but were sealed out of it. Particularly, I would say, the community-based grassroots training people. There was no process, no structure by which they could be included. When collective bargaining happens in our unions, at some point a few people go off in a room, knock heads and eventually bring out a tentative agreement. The members' choice is whether to ratify it or not. This very exclusive process is understood by most of our membership, but it's unfamiliar and distasteful to many of our social allies. So if we are involved in social bargaining, we have to figure how to open up the process.

As the bargaining continued, we did brief Bob Rae's office, and the Ontario NDP caucus. By the day the final report was released, with three labour signatures, we had a full scale, 30-page OFL critique available at the press conference. So I think we kept some of our perspective and some of our balance. But this was a major commitment of staff time over several months. We can manage that once or twice in a year, at most. In this case, the shift from side track to express lane was made by over-extending union technical staff, pushing our intellectual allies to the limit, and excluding most social movements with whom we need to work in coalition. The final text was remarkably progressive, but the achievement on paper was very costly in political process.

There are lots more policy processes ahead if we really tackle the provincial training issue. If effective participation drains our limited resources, we need to be clear on which government and employer initiatives we participate in. We only had three labour people directly on the Premier's Council. But at the same time, unionists were participating in CLMPC (Canadian Labour Market Productivity Centre) processes, and in joint task forces on this and that. There are not clear channels about how all that gets resolved. It is the jurisdiction of the central labour bodies to make these decisions, but often choices are made under time pressure and the number of these structures is multiplying. They are like amoebas, there are millions of them and they divide into millions more sub-committees.

Consider how few people there are in any affiliate who could carry on an informed discussion around training policy in Ontario. What we need is about 500 unionists who could carry on that discussion and we don't have them yet. I think we need to acknowledge this "skill shortage" and resolve it.

Once we broaden the number of people involved, we can better handle the divergencies of views within our movement on training questions. I think frequently that the differences within the movement on training policy are treated as ideological differences: so and so is in a radical fantasyland; so and so is in bed with government or management. But most of the time these divergent positions are about differences of jurisdictions, differences of sector, differences of bargaining leverage and strength, differences of sophistication and depth in staff, differences in regional base. Those differences are as important as the ideological ones and they can only find their proper place when we have 500 union experts in the province, all actively listening to the diverse voices of the membership.

Tensions In The Union Culture

Training highlights some of the structural tensions in union life. Let me suggest how the de-centralized, collective and subordinate ethos of unions cause trouble when we're engaged in training.

First, most union negotiating in Ontario is de-centralized, while the benefits of training are diffused widely. Coordinated bargaining in the private sector has been systematically attacked by employers, while privatization and re-structuring have divided bargaining units in the public sector. Yet the benefits of enhanced job skills often aren't felt at a single workplace. In an increasingly volatile labour market, many workers upgrade themselves in one job, only to move to another workplace, where the skills may or may not be put to full use. This means that employers and co-workers have a limited stake in bargaining local training clauses and making them work.

Secondly, the collective dynamic of unionism often clashes with the way individual workers learn. Training isn't a benefit like severance pay or pensions, easily quantified and regulated. Learning is essentially a voluntary act, intimately linked to personal motivation. As the issue of streaming in schools has shown, simply ensuring equal access to a study program provides little assurance of equity in outcomes. We can succeed, for example, in ensuring that all employees in a workplace receive a week of training on computer literacy. But if a worker has no basic math, no typing experience, a back ailment and an unemployed spouse, their experience of that week will be utterly different from a co-worker whose situation is different. Because educational capital, like financial capital, tends to concentrate, the challenge of equity in training is profound. It will require sensitive counselling, democratized design process and a broad range of choices for individuals and groups within workplaces. None of these are easy to institutionalize, nor is equity in outcomes easy to regulate.

Thirdly, the subordinate status of unions limits our effectiveness as a training vehicle for our members. Employers don't share what they know about future plans for the workplace. At this point, we lack the skills and resources to profile and address the diverse learning needs and learning styles of our members. As a result, we lack the two key tools for effective educational planning... knowledge of needed future skills and of the learners.

Until this changes, "planning" for training will be dominated by the employers. We know it is fruitless to lecture Third

World countries about the importance of economic planning, when they can't regulate either imports or exports of goods and capital. Similarly, it's misleading to set up union head offices as training planners, unless the resources, skills and mandate are developed which could make us effective planners.

We should be sobered by the ways our de-centralized, collective and subordinate dynamics limit the way we function. As we exhort companies and governments to change, we must be willing to change ourselves. And that's easier said than done.

How do we overcome the fragmentation of collective bargaining over training? Union mergers, sectoral agreements and legislative entitlements are possible elements in this task. How do we develop the delicate, precise supports needed for empowerment of individual member/learners in often rigid union structures? From union counselling we have some experience that can help us. How do we ensure the clout, skill and information flow needed to work as genuine equals with management and educational institutions in structuring training opportunities? From our safety and health joint committees, we can draw some lessons.

What role will there be for employer input on training into this government? I think that it is fairly clear what the channels are for us to have input into this government. But we have to face a fact. We may not like the employers with whom we deal. We may be frustrated when they go out pursuing their own interests. But we should not be surprised. And a government of this province has to deal with business. Are they going to deal with business through the back door, or are they going to deal with us there?

We can say we don't want to be a part of that. We can tell the NDP to go on ahead and get their hands dirty, while we deal with business only across the bargaining table. I submit that the process of social bargaining is one in which we need to remain involved. How we do it in a way that includes the rank and file of our movement and our social allies is, I think, the interesting question. But because the government is 'our' government does not mean that we are the only people they have to listen to.

Employers have been coming at us like 18-wheelers, with all kinds of initiatives. Around training, around workplace reorganization, around new technology, around high commitment systems and so on. What Dave Robertson used to call the three T's — training, tech change and team concept. But I think the momentum is shifting. With shutdowns, free trade losses and cutbacks, Ontario management's confidence is being shaken.

As an internally diverse movement, with some underlying principles and some solid street smarts, we are facing a whole new terrain of challenge. It is appropriate for us to be very cautious about how we handle ourselves. Many training offers are poison pills. But our members want training. Up until now, most of them have been told by the labour leadership that more training is good, the way to get ahead.

So we have a floating crap game in training. And in Ontario, the most interesting game right now is being played at the provincial level. We have an NDP government and very solid policy work done within the OFL. We have our internal tensions and our limited resources, but we also have a great chance to move the line forward. Let's not blow it.

D'Arcy Martin is a National Representative with the Communications and Electrical Workers of Canada (CWC).

Chapter Seven

Training Needs: An Objective Science?
Nancy Jackson

In these few brief pages I want to try to tackle some of the beliefs about training that we have previously treated as good common sense ... and good business practice. Among them are the ideas that training needs are a *practical empirical* problem, and that they can be satisfactorily determined through *objective, rational/scientific* methods of investigation and decision-making.

Perhaps on the face of it, these seem like simple enough claims, and anyway, you may ask, if training needs are not a practical problem with a rational solution, then why would we waste any time on it?

Granted, my basic point here is not exactly an easy one. But I will try to be concrete and take it one step at a time. Obviously I do think a realistic approach to training needs assessment can be found. But, as you will see, I think we need to considerably broaden our procedures.

An Outdated Logic

The general theme of my criticisms may be familiar, because my target is the kind of logic we have inherited from a century of scientific management. That is, we have learned that a rational/ systematic approach to problem-solving is the only defensible method of doing business. We have learned that such an approach is not only good business, but indeed it is just good common sense in any kind of venture. Goals are to specified in advance, in clear and precise detail. Making goals explicit and concrete means outcomes can be more certain. Everyone can see what is expected and can tell whether the objectives are being reached. This approach makes supervision possible and accountability reasonable because everything is visible and agreed upon in advance. It is a familiar story ...

This kind of logic is very persuasive, but little by little we are being torn away from the hold it has had on us in the workplace. New management methods are increasingly challenging this basic logic as a way to organize a labour process, if we want to maximize the working potential of human beings. I want to argue that it also provides a poor way to understand training needs, and over the next few pages I will try to show you some of the reasons why this might be true.

Under the heading of "rational/systematic/scientific" approaches to training needs I would include most of what is currently done under the banner of "competency-based needs analysis" and "curriculum design." I recognize the enormous popularity of this approach, and grant not only that it is one possible way to define training needs, but indeed one that has the virtue of producing some answers quite quickly. However, the important question is, what kind of answers? What is the quality of the information it gives us? Does this method of proceeding identify the right problems? Does it ask the right questions? Does it examine the right evidence? Does it advocate solutions that will really make a difference, or will they reproduce in future the same problems that we are struggling with today?

My answers to most of these questions are not very favourable. That is why I think the alternatives we are looking for will not be found through minor innovations or adjustments in our methods. Rather I think we are in need of a major overhaul, a fresh approach. I will come back to the business of alternatives, but first let me be more specific about some criticisms.

Four Fabulous Fictions

I have identified what I will call "four fabulous fictions" of the rational approach to needs analysis: 'fabulous' because they are so attractive, and we want to believe in them; fictions because in the end, they don't stand the test of reality. Of necessity, I will give overly brief and rough sketches, but I hope you will be able to recognize the problems I have in mind. You will also see that I am thinking here about issues related to skills training for waged employees rather than management training.

FICTION ONE is that the identification of training needs must take the form of clear, precise, detailed specification of performance goals in measurable terms. This is the basic axiom that is most often associated with good common sense. Furthermore, this axiom rests on the belief that what workers most need to learn is specific tasks or performance specifications that will improve their contribution to productivity.

Well, the first problem with all this precision is that it offers the seductive suggestion of simplicity where none may exist. It cleans up real life complexities and ambiguities, and in the process, gives us a bargain which, in the end, maybe we can't afford. In fact I would argue that our workplaces today are full of ambiguities, only a few of which I will be able to mention here. In this context, clear, precise, even measurable training goals geared to specific tasks and job functions may be exactly the wrong way to go.

In fact, in many of today's jobs, it is increasingly less clear what might radically improve productivity. A simple story based on work in an office environment will make my point. It is a story from a task-analysis workshop I attended a few years ago in B.C. where employers were gathered to analyze their training requirements for entry level secretarial or office administration staff. There were many hours of debate about how much and what kind of preparation these young women should be given. At one point, the discussion focussed for a while on the growing use of spreadsheets in the office, and the question became how students could be trained to use a spreadsheet efficiently. Different employers had quite different views about this question, as you will see from the following comment:

> "I think a knowledge of what they are doing will increase their speed, as opposed to having to type faster .... Say, if you are using a spread sheet package. How quickly you finish the spreadsheet doesn't depend upon how quickly you type. It depends on your approach and your knowledge of how the package works."

These employers had a hard time deciding whether what made a good entry level secretary was someone with good typing speed and accuracy, or one with a good general knowledge of business, of basic accounting principles and of computing software. In the end, they decided that while what they really wanted was the latter, they might settle for the former. The question is, was that a good training choice, and why? Maybe by moving on to my next points, possible answers to this question will come into focus.

FICTION TWO is the idea that the necessary or desirable levels of training — what is sometimes called "sufficiency" — can be decided by carefully analysing current jobs found in our workplaces.

I have two general problems with this reasoning. The first is with its present-tense focus. That is, using existing jobs as the unit of analysis locks us into the present in ways that may not serve anyone very well. There are at least two reasons. One is that jobs have futures — they are changing, more rapidly all the time. So their requirements change, and since training, by definition, is always for the future, then the present may not be a very appropriate benchmark for future needs.

Secondly, people have futures, too. The minimum that an individual needs to know to perform today's job, or even the minimum she needs to know to perform tomorrow's job — may not provide an adequate basis for her long term value to the firm once she has acquired a range of basic experience.

Again, let me emphasize this dilemma with the words of another employer from the task-analysis workshop in B.C. This time, the quotation comes from a debate about a whether a program for entry level office workers should include instruction in public speaking.

"Well, I think they need good communication skills even at entry level. Because if you get a young person coming in who can't even talk in the interview ... then you know this person may be good for six months in the job but then that's it. They won't go any further."

This employer was from an accounting firm that made it a policy not to hire anyone — even an entry-level data entry clerk — who couldn't grow with the firm.

My next objection to the focus on current jobs is that even if we can figure out how they could be performed better, that may not be the source of the greatest improvements in the workplace. Maybe what is needed is a whole new approach to designing and organizing work. Spending a fortune to improve performance in a job that is poorly conceived or designed in the first place is short-sighted.... spending good money after bad.

In fact, an increasingly large percentage of changes being considered by employers involve re-organization of work flow and job assignment rather than just tinkering with procedures. Any form of needs analysis that has to wait until after the job is in place, so that it can focus on specific procedures for performance, offers too little, too late. It means that training will always be reactive and limited in its vision. Again, I would ask, is this the most effective way we can find to think about training?

FICTION THREE is the notion that highly specific, performance-oriented training goals can be identified that will fit a broad range of workplaces.

This claim is especially attractive where training is designed to serve more than one employer, such as through a community college. But it is a troublesome point on a number of levels.

The underlying assumption here is that training needs are derivable from technology, materials, and productions processes in use in a given sector. Because there are consistencies in these elements between workplaces, we expect to find similarities in skill requirements. But if we look more closely, we find this logic is not very useful as a guide to training design, for several reasons.

Firstly, although there are indeed consistencies across the

electrical sector as elsewhere, we also find considerable variety in the technologies, materials, production processes and work organization methods in use. Variety exists not only between companies but even within single workplaces, for example where several generations of technology exist alongside one another, reflecting a conversion process that is incremental rather than revolutionary. In such a workplace, skill requirements may indeed vary, from workshop to workshop, or office to office, within the same firm.

Secondly, skill requirements are not determined by technologies and materials, and production processes alone. They are determined by human choices about the methods of implementation and organization of these elements. And in these areas of choice, we almost always find significant variation between workplaces. So for example, the same production line will be staffed differently, or the same technical breakdown will be handled by different people and procedures, depending on local conditions, collective agreements and management methods. As a result, we find a corresponding difference in the actual skill requirements between workplaces, and thus different immediate "needs" in performance-oriented training.

Methods of needs analysis which abstract from these differences to a mythical "typical workplace" create, in fact, a workplace that doesn't quite exist and a set of performance requirements that don't quite fit anyone's circumstances in real life. This leads to at least two lines of questioning. Are these mythical performance requirements really a good basis for training design? Or, conversely, would good training design in these circumstances really focus on specific performance requirements? What would be the alternative?

FICTION FOUR is the idea that training needs determined in a systematic and thorough manner will be unbiased, impartial, or neutral.

I have argued in the last few pages that training 'needs' are always relative to choices — choices about technology and work organization. And choices are always relative to goals — both short- and long-term priorities in the workplace. So, in the end, the goals underlying production choices go a long way toward determining whether the training 'needs' will be impartial.

Every assembly line worker in this country can tell the difference between partial and impartial training. If training to streamline work routines makes the line move faster in the name of efficiency and productivity, and leads to increased eyestrain, back pain and fatigue at the end of the day, it's clear whose side the training is on. The only alternative to this win/lose game is to explicitly recognize the needs of workers for improved working conditions as distinct from, and of equal importance to, the needs of management for improved productivity. Only when we explicitly, publicly, and jointly make it our goal to balance these two sets of interests we will have training "needs" that are impartial. That will only happen if we develop and enforce these goals as a condition of doing business in Canada. In the Canada of the 1990s, we are a long way from realizing this ideal.

Meanwhile, the practice of superimposing a set of rational/scientific procedures on decisions about training needs, in the name of objectivity and impartiality, amounts to a highly political act. It provides a cloak of apparently neutral rationality under which intensely political choices go unexamined and unchallenged.

A Question Of Alternatives

It must be clear by now that I think there are reasonable alternatives for thinking about training, but that they start from a very different place than the methods we mostly use today.

They start with the recognition that the specification of requirements for training is ultimately an interpretive rather than empirical problem, a matter of 'choice' rather than 'science.' Training options are part of a larger choice between differing strategies of work organization and production relations, and such choices are fundamentally social and political in character. Indeed, the impact of these choices is felt well beyond the workplace, because when we choose how people will work, we are also choosing how they will live, and shaping the kind of society which we will have.

Alternative approaches to training involve recognizing that there is more than one set of 'needs' embedded in work and that a productive and stable workforce can result only from recognizing and addressing this diversity. Good training in this context would, of necessity, focus on more than specific performance requirements. Instead, it would grow out of longer-term commitment to both individual and industrial futures.

I recognize that a training system based on this kind of thinking can't be built overnight. Training systems with a broad, long term vision weren't built overnight in other parts of the industrialized world — in Germany, Sweden, or Japan — where they are nevertheless in use today. But, in Canada, we are at a fork in the road, and we have a choice to make. Will we follow the logic of the last century into the future and just hope for the best? Or will we find the courage to change our ways and build a training system that truly serves our needs — as corporations, as individuals, and as a society?

I would like to bring you one more quotation from British Columbia, even though some of you may have heard it before. This time the words are from a technology instructor in one of the community colleges, who spoke to me about his own students in a competency-based auto mechanics class. He reflected somewhat wistfully on the contradictions he felt turning them out into the labour market. His remarks capture for me quite simply the nature of the larger dilemma we have created for ourselves as a society by opting for 'quick fixes' in training. He said:

> "These students can perform discrete mechanical repair tasks ... but they've got no feel for the engine. I wouldn't want to hire them in my garage!"

Nancy Jackson is Co-Managing Director of the Automotive Parts Sectoral Training Council and Assistant Professor in the Faculty of Education at McGill University.

Appendices

UNION POLICIES AND CONTRACT LANGUAGE ON JOB TRAINING

Appendix I

Education and Training

A POLICY ADOPTED AT THE 33rd ANNUAL CONVENTION OF THE ONTARIO FEDERATION OF LABOUR, NOVEMBER, 1989

Introduction

Employers and governments are engaging in a lot of double talk about training. On the one hand, they have mounted a campaign to convince the public that the future of our jobs and our country depends on training workers. They describe the minds and skills of workers as Canada's most fundamental natural resource that will be increasingly crucial as industries become more technologically sophisticated and knowledge-intensive.

On the other hand, the same employers and governments are pursuing economic policies (free trade, deregulation, privatization) that are stripping Canada of good-paying, skilled, full-time jobs. These are being replaced primarily with low-paying, less-skilled and often part-time jobs.

The federal government — the government mainly responsible for financing training — has cut back significantly on its support for training.

At corporate urging, governments are cutting back on funds to public educational institutions — the backbone of Canada's training system.

Also with active corporate support, governments have all but eliminated their traditional initiatives for new job creation. Such initiatives are necessary if people newly entering or re-entering the labour force are to have good-paying, secure jobs.

The new corporate emphasis on training has two roots. One is the dwindling of traditional sources of trained workers — immigrants and young people. The other is the need for workers to adjust to the massive transformation of economic life. This transformation is being caused by corporate global reorganization — of which free trade, privatization, deregulation and new technologies are part.

As training becomes more of a public issue, it is essential that the labour movement in Ontario be clear about our agenda for training. It is very different from the corporate agenda.

In the following sections of this policy paper, we will discuss:

- labour's training agenda
- ending discrimination
- different activities that get confused in discussions of skills training
- guidelines for good skills training
- the need to reject the privatization of skills training in favour of a public training model in which labour has a significant voice
- the ways in which skills training is to be funded
- local union structures and skills training
- labour's action plan

Labour's Training Agenda

We want training that equips workers to have more control

over their jobs and their work lives, builds on workers' existing capabilities, prepares workers for what they want and need to know now and in the future, puts workers in a better position to shape that future and starts eliminating job discrimination based on gender, race or ethnicity.

We also want training that leads to good jobs. We know training only makes sense when it is part of an economic strategy for full employment, for the creation of good-paying secure jobs and for a labour process which relies on workers' skills rather than one which tries to dispense with the skills and the workers.

The employers' training agenda is to make workers more willing and able cogs in the corporate machine.

The differences in our training agendas are related to our differences on education. The trade union movement has fought for many years for an educational system that is open to everyone, non-elitist in its operation, relevant to the life-long needs of workers and their children, and equips everyone with the skills and knowledge to function fully in their lives at work, at home and in the community.

Job-skills training is part of the educational process and must be run in a manner consistent with our broader educational goals.

Labour's recognition of the difference between the labour and corporate agendas for training and education led the Ontario Federation of Labour and its affiliates to set up BEST (Basic Education for Skills Training) — labour's own literacy and second-language program. We had had enough of adult basic education programs that saw their mandate, as a recent Laubach Literacy of Canada leaflet describes its purpose, "To make employees more valuable to employers."

It is time we went further in our initiatives. It is time the trade union movement developed a policy and plan of action that will help achieve more and better skills training, consistent with the needs of workers.

Ending Discrimination

Education and training in Canada have been discriminatory for many years. In the educational system, many working class children are streamed into the dead-end programs.[1] Their more affluent counterparts are directed almost automatically to academic programs leading to post-secondary education and good paying jobs.

Discrimination has also been a feature of workplace-related training. Programs leading to the best jobs have been primarily the preserve of white men. The most obvious example is apprenticeship where the percentage of women in programs other than cooking and hairdressing is tiny. The pattern is similar in other training programs that are considered desirable.

Women who are attempting to re-enter the paid labour force are usually slotted into low-paying, less-skilled jobs.

Correcting these discriminatory practices in education and training will not be easy, but it must be done. A starting point is labour's belief that all Canadians have a right to a good basic education, defined as Grade 12 or its equivalent.

For those who have been denied that education, for whatever reason, opportunities must be provided to catch up. These opportunities must assure people the necessary income to live while studying. They must assure employed workers the time to catch up and protection of their jobs while doing so. They must assure all adults that their knowledge and skills will be respected.

Similarly, job-skills training programs must be structured to correct the exclusion of women and visible minorities. Since women still are made to bear the main responsibility for children, it is essential that good, accessible child care be provided.

Other barriers facing women also must be dealt with: lack of information about training opportunities, low self-esteem from past discriminatory practices, lack of adequate income support, little opportunity to update basic educational skills, spousal opposition, and lack of good job opportunities following training.

The pattern of discrimination against visible minorities is maintained by many of the same barriers, compounded by a

---

1. For a discussion of this issue, see *Stacking The Deck: The Streaming of Working Class Kids In Ontario Schools*, published in 1992 by Our Schools/Our Selves, Toronto.

pattern of institutionalized racism which closes doors to good education and training programs, and blocks access to good jobs even when access to training is gained.

Every training program must measure its design in terms of how it proposes to overcome hurdles to fairness and equality.

Who Employers Train And For What

While employers are touting the importance of training, survey after survey shows that only a minority of employers engage in any training.

The latest Statistics Canada survey indicated that only one out of four employers provided training. This is consistent with recent data from the Ontario Ministry of Skills Development.

When discussing training, however, it is important to distinguish many different activities employers call training.

One is skills training — training whose purpose is to acquire the knowledge and abilities to work. To the extent that employers do skills training, it tends to be for management, sales staff and some technical workers such as engineers.

When non-management workers do receive training from employers, it tends not to be skills training. Rather, it is usually orientation training ("here are the rules," "there is the washroom") or cultural training (directed to shaping the way workers think about the employer, the need to be competitive, to work cooperatively with management, etc.)

The focus of this paper is on skills training.

For employed workers, most formal skills training continues to be provided in one of two ways: apprenticeship programs for the traditional trades and public education programs for everyone else. (Ontario's community colleges provide the in-school portion of apprenticeship training as well.)

Whatever additional skills training most workers receive, it is informal training provided by co-workers on the job. We should not minimize the importance of informal training. It is training that addresses workers' real needs and is based on the experience of people who know the job. Most workers end up being both learners and trainers in this informal training network on the job. Our experience in informal training makes us aware of what we want from formal training programs. It also helps us be more knowledgeable about what kinds of education and training are effective.

Skills Training For Displaced Workers And New Entrants

However limited employed workers find their job-training opportunities, displaced workers (who have lost jobs because of layoffs or closures) have even fewer good skills training opportunities. New entrants (people preparing to enter or re-enter the labour force) have a mixture of training opportunities. Labour's training agenda must deal with the needs of all three groups.

Guidelines For Good Training

There are certain common principles that must guide all skills training — whether for employed workers, displaced workers or new entrants.

These general guidelines are:

1. Skills training must be developmental. Every training program must teach skills in a way that goes beyond a particular job and leaves the trainee better able to take on different tasks in the future. This must be the case whether the program lasts two hours or two years.
2. Skills training programs must be open to all, not just the youngest or fittest. Special efforts must be made to use training as a vehicle for equality for women, visible minorities and others who have been discriminated against in the educational system and the workplace.
3. Skills training must be designed to raise the level of skill of the entire workforce, not just selected occupations or selected areas.
4. Skills training must flow from a worker-based identification of skill needs and not be restricted to narrowly-defined job performance factors identified by employers or consultants.
5. Skills training must support the development of good job

design and technology that enhance the skills of workers.
6. Skills training must equip the trainee to be better able to have more control over his/her work.
7. Skills training must incorporate the practices of good adult education. It must start with what trainees know and want to know. It must respect abilities people bring to the training. It must use active learning techniques that make trainees' questions central. It must encourage questioning, discussion and participation.
8. Skills training must incorporate information that helps the trainee work safely, learn about individual and collective rights and be better equipped to put one's knowledge and experience into action.

There are additional guidelines for specific groups of trainees:

For Employed Workers:

1. All workers must have the right to skills training and upgrading as part of the job.
2. Skills training entitlements have to be accumulated in guaranteed and measurable terms — such as days per worker per year.
3. Skills training must be conducted during working hours and without other work pressures.
4. Labour must have a significant role in determining the goals, content and delivery of skills training programs.
5. Separate from and in addition to skills training, every worker must be entitled to accumulated credits (days per year) for paid educational leave to be spent as the worker wishes.

Canada must ratify the International Labour Organization Convention 140 on paid educational leave which recognizes workers' rights to paid educational leave for "training at any level; general, social and civic education; and trade union education."

For Displaced Workers:

1. Training opportunities must be available to all displaced workers.

2. Accessibility must be assured by government provision of adequate income support and social support services such as child care and counselling.
3. Workers must be able to refer themselves to training programs they wish to enter.
4. Training must be directed to providing real skills, not trying to shape workers expectations so they are more willing to take poor-paying, insecure jobs.
5. All programs must be provided in conjunction with public educational institutions.

For New Entrants:

1. Training must be open to all.
2. Accessibility must be assured by government provision of adequate income support and social support services such as child care and counselling.
3. Training initiatives must be coordinated among the three levels of government and among the ministries within each level of government.
4. Training must be directed to providing real skills, not trying to shape the attitudes of new entrants passively to accept the poor-quality, poor-paying jobs that are the focus for most "entry-level" training.
5. Training must address the varying needs of people entering or re-entering the workforce: there are specific problems for women attempting to return to paid work after years outside the labour force, as there are for the disabled and for the long-term unemployed.
6. All training programs must be provided in conjunction with public educational institutions.

Apprenticeship Training:

Apprenticeship training, which combines elements of employed-worker training and new-entrant training, has some unique aspects that must guide its operation:

1. The current "time-based" programs, that provide an

adequate period for the apprentice to learn from the journey person, must continue and not be replaced by a "competency-based" approach.

So-called "competency-based" training assumes that all the skills a tradesperson needs can be identified, listed and tested. It takes training out of the relationship between the journey person and apprentice. It denies that all trades are an art and a science. It fails to recognize that there is no substitute for experience which only comes with time.

2. The in-school portion of training must continue to be interspersed with practical experience in the workplace.

Many potential apprentices welcome the chance to get education and training that starts with practical work and introduces "theory" after having had experience. They would be less likely to participate in apprenticeship training if the academic portion were put at the beginning.

It also would turn the colleges into agencies that sort out people before employers have to make a commitment to the apprentice. Such sorting on academic grounds is not necessarily the basis on which to decide who will be a good tradesperson.

3. Apprenticeship training must become accessible to all.

This will require continued pre-apprenticeship familiarization programs. It will require better efforts to acquaint guidance counsellors and other youth advisers with information about apprenticeship training. It also will require increased government support for apprenticeships to expand the number of places. Finally, it will require new programs to target existing women and visible minority employees as potential apprentices with their current employers.

Affirmative action targets must be set and employers must be pressed to undertake apprenticeship training.

Public, Not Private

The guidelines and principles for skills training cannot be separated from the mechanism for delivering that training.

Labour can only achieve its agenda for worker-centred, accessible, equitable, and developmental skills training when training is conducted in conjunction with public educational institutions in which labour has a much more significant voice than it does now.

The labour movement in Canada has been very clear that privatization of public services is contrary to workers' interests. Privatization of education and training is a particular concern.

Through many years of experience, the labour movement knows that private sector trainers will not consistently deliver the kind of training we want. Their focus is on the short-term bottom line, on bending workers and work practices to employers' goals, on providing just-in-time skills in an increasingly replaceable work force.

However much advocacy of training is part of the corporate message these days; corporate training practices now and in the past speak louder than words.

We believe public educational institutions are the best alternative. In conjunction with labour and business, they can provide training programs on the job as well as at the school, college or university.

Unlike employer-run training programs, public educational institutions:

> offer the possibility of public accountability and control; orient to learners as their clients, not as means to other ends; have no vested interest in restricting the scope of training only to what meets a narrow, employer-specified task requirement.

To achieve their full potential, public educational institutions must become more responsive to workers and workers' needs. Curriculum and teaching practices must be stripped of anti-labour bias where it exists.

Expertise in training developed by labour and others in the community must be drawn into the colleges and other public educational institutions. This will allow them to become a more broad-based community focal point for learning. There are already some attempts to achieve this goal in school boards and colleges. George Brown College in Toronto, for example, has set up a community outreach program that provides training in conjunction with labour, community groups and business.

Ontario's network of secondary and post-secondary educational institutions is among the most extensive in the industrialized world. It makes no practical or economic sense to bypass or abandon these institutions. We must not attempt to invent new vehicles to provide skills training nor try to import training models from other countries where the history and context are different. We must make a commitment to our existing public institutions and change them so they better meet our broader educational and training needs.

The use of public educational institutions as the vehicle for skills training does raise two issues — funding and control.

Good training is expensive. Public educational institutions will not be able to provide that training adequately unless governments reverse their cutbacks in support for skills training. Substantially more training requires substantially more financial resources.

The parallel issue is control. Although public educational institutions offer the possibility of public control, they are often set up in a way that there is little genuine public voice in their operation. Changes are necessary.

Labour's Role In Public Educational Institutions

School boards are elected and there is a genuine opportunity for public control. Community colleges and universities are governed by appointed boards that reflect a small and unrepresentative sector of the public. Almost all appointees to these boards are well-to-do and directly or indirectly represent the business community.

As a result, colleges and universities tend to ignore the broad needs of the community. Their policies, educational programs and operating procedures often fail to respond to the needs of working people.

To correct this, governance of these institutions must be turned over to boards that are genuinely represent the diverse interests of labour, business, other groups within the community and teachers, support staff and students.

This goal can be achieved by provincial government action to change the board appointment procedure. Each college and university must have a board composed of external and internal members. One third of the external board members must represent labour. There should be an equal number representing business and an equal number representing the community in its diversity. In addition, there should be internal board members representing the institution's teachers, support staff and students. Each of the external and internal groups must nominate their own representatives to be appointed.

The Ministry of Colleges and Universities must provide funding so that board members will be reimbursed for expenses and wages lost while undertaking board duties. Boards can have a full complement of labour and genuine community representatives only when such funding is available.

An effective labour voice in local, publicly-elected school boards will require a new commitment from the trade union movement. Public education and training issues will have to be raised more regularly within local unions. Local unions will have to help their members get more active in parent associations and school councils. Equally important, the trade union movement will have to take school board elections more seriously. We must encourage trade unionists to be candidates, help fund campaigns and make sure a labour viewpoint is expressed.

More substantial labour representation on boards will provide an opportunity. We must be prepared to seize that opportunity to achieve good education and training for workers and for future workers. Our training guidelines, previously noted, provide the blueprint we need.

Funding

The source of funding for skills training should vary depending on whether the training is for employed, displaced or new labour force entrants.

Employed Workers

Skills training for employed workers should be funded by

employers through a provincial payroll training tax. The money raised through the training tax should be administered by a newly-created Ontario training commission. It should be composed half of labour representatives and half of business representatives. One co-chairperson should be chosen by each group.

The Ontario training commission should have the sole power to authorize expenditures from the training tax fund.

Funding should be available only to commission-approved skills training programs run through public educational institutions. Labour would use its 50 percent control of the commission to assure that program approval would be dependent on skills training programs meeting labour's training program criteria.

Current employer expenditures for approved apprenticeship programs also should be funded by the commission with training tax funds. The in-school portion of apprenticeship training should continue to be funded by government.

Displaced Workers

Labour is outraged by the failure of the federal and Ontario governments to provide adequately for displaced workers. The Ontario government's Industrial Restructuring Commission is a sham. It consists of a single commissioner, with no labour participation, and does nothing but watch as workers are thrown onto the street as a result of the free trade deal. The needs of displaced workers are great. Decisive action must be taken: the training component is essential.

Training for displaced workers should be provided through government-financed training programs run in conjunction with public educational institutions.

Income support should be provided to allow displaced workers to participate in training.

The money should come from Unemployment Insurance or from a government income support program for those ineligible for UI benefits. Displaced workers should be assured of 90 percent of their previous wage levels.

Funding for social support services (child care, medical and dental coverage, transportation. counselling) for trainees must be increased. The provincial government should take the lead in attempting to coordinate these programs offered by the three levels of government.

Benefits for UI recipients and income support program recipients must:

- be available for up to 156 weeks of training;
- allow recipients to refer themselves to categories of training;
- not be required to satisfy job search requirements;
- not be subjected to a waiting period before they can participate in a training program;
- not be required to treat severance benefits and pension income as earnings that count against UI benefits or training support allowances.

New Entrants

Training programs for people preparing to enter or re-enter the labour force should be funded directly by the federal and provincial governments through public educational institutions.

Adequate income support must be an integral part of the program and funded through a federal-provincial training income support program.

Funding for social support services (child care, medical and dental coverage, transportation, counselling) for trainees must be increased. The provincial government should take the lead in attempting to coordinate these programs offered by the three levels of government.

New direct job creation programs must be undertaken by federal, provincial and municipal governments to provide secure, good-paying jobs into which new workers can enter.

Local Union Involvement

Labour is calling for a significant role in determining the goals, content and delivery of skills training programs for employed workers. We want funding allocated through an Ontario training commission in which we have half the members. We want a more significant say in the operation of community college and university boards.

While we are pressing for these changes, it is very important to establish local union structures to bring training needs of workers forward and to bring information back to workers about training opportunities.

A system of local union education representatives meets this need. These education representatives could be members of existing local union education committees or they could be newly created positions. They should not be people who are instructors since the demands of the two jobs are different and each is time-consuming. Education representatives in each workplace would be responsible for:

- helping articulate workers' training needs in that workplace;
- assisting the local union leadership in identifying and helping design programs to meet those needs;
- conveying information about existing training opportunities;
- representing the local union in meetings of education representatives from other workplaces to share information and ideas to advance workers' educational and training opportunities and programs.

Labour's Action Plan

1. The OFL (Ontario Federation of Labour) will step up its pressure on the Ontario government for the introduction of a training tax (based on payroll) to fund skills training for employed workers. The proceeds of this tax are to be administered by a bi-partite Ontario training commission for commission-approved programs run in conjunction with public educational institutions.

2. The OFL will continue to press for changes in the structure of the boards of governors of colleges and universities. Each institution's board should consist of an equal number of external members representing labour, business and the community. In addition, there should continue to be internal board members representing the institution's teachers, support staff and students.

3. The OFL will promote union involvement in school board activities and in school trustee elections.
4. The OFL will prepare materials to inform school boards, colleges, universities, employers and governments about labour's guidelines for good skills training. The OFL will work to see that these guidelines are incorporated in all training programs.
5. The OFL Education Department will organize a conference in 1990 to discuss training-related issues. It will focus on employed workers, displaced workers and people preparing to enter or re-enter the labour force.
6. The OFL Education Department will work with affiliates to develop materials and guidelines for local union education representatives.

Summary – Education And Training Policy Paper

Employers and governments are engaging in a lot of double talk about training. They claim training is the key to Canada's economic future.

But their economic policies (free trade, deregulation, privatization) are stripping Canada of good-paying, skilled, full-time jobs and replacing them with low-paying, less-skilled and often part-time jobs. The federal government has cut its spending on training and, like the Ontario government, has all but eliminated funds for job creation.

Training is not a substitute for a full-employment policy that will produce secure, well-paying jobs. Nor is training a substitute for a labour adjustment program that provides alternative jobs, income support and supportive social programs.

Training is important as long as it accompanies such programs and as long as it is worker-driven. The key elements of a labour view of training are:

1. Training is a right. This right must be universal — available without barriers to all employed workers, displaced workers and people wanting to enter or re-enter the work force.
2. Training is a tool for greater equity. It is an instrument for overcoming the particular inequities in the labour market

APPENDIX I

faced by women, visible minorities, native Canadians, the disabled, and immigrants.
3. Training is a fundamental part of the job. Employed workers must have access to training during working hours with full pay. Displaced workers and those entering the work force must have access to training with income support and necessary support services such as child care and counselling.
4. Training rights include the opportunity, through paid educational leave, for workers to upgrade themselves to achieve a high school education.
5. The content of training must be geared to workers' needs as they see them and must be developmental. Skills must be taught in a way that goes beyond a particular job and leaves trainees better able to take on different tasks in the future. Training must increase workers' control over technology and their work.
6. Workers and their unions must have a central role in determining, at all levels, the direction of training.
7. Training for employed workers should be funded by a new training tax on employers. The funds raised by this tax should be administered by a newly-created Ontario training commission composed equally of labour and business representatives.
8. Training for displaced workers and people wishing to enter or re-enter the labour force should be funded out of general revenue. There should be income support provided by an enriched UI program or by a new income support program for those ineligible for UI. Social support services also must be provided.
9. Training programs must be carried out in conjunction with public education in situations in which labour has a much more significant voice. These institutions may have to modify their own structures and approaches, but they are an invaluable resource suited to channeling training in a broader direction, sensitive to the needs of workers as clients, and accountable to the public.

Appendix II

We Can Do It: Invest In Training And Restore U.I.

**A POLICY PAPER ADOPTED AT
THE 19th CONSTITUTIONAL CONVENTION
OF THE CANADIAN LABOUR CONGRESS,
JUNE, 1989**

1. Canadian workers are going through the worst crisis since the Great Depression.
2. Tory economic mismanagement in the form of the Free Trade Agreement, privatization, deregulation, the GST and a host of other regressive economic policies have had a devastating impact on workers across the nation. The result has been massive layoffs, plant closures, soaring bankruptcies, a hard hit retail sector and public sector layoffs pushing the "official" unemployment rate to over 10 percent, representing 1.5 million jobless Canadians.
3. This crisis is even worse than the severe economic downturn of 1982. This time, most of the layoffs are permanent. The regressive policy direction of the Tory government over

the last eight years has created an overwhelming need for effective, quality adjustment programs. Yet, this government has failed to deliver, leaving millions of Canadians to experience the devastation of unemployment, underemployment and poverty.

4. As bad as it is, the "official" monthly unemployment rate does not even begin to tell the whole story. It excludes the tens of thousands who have given up looking for work each month because none is available. It does not indicate the distress of more than 500,000 part-time workers who want and need full-time jobs. It does not show that full-time workers have been forced to work shorter hours or job share. Had these been included, the real unemployment rate would have been over 15 percent, 50 percent higher than the "officially" reported rate. Even that does not show that up to one-third of the workforce experiences unemployment at some time during the year.

5. The "official" employment statistics do not show that if decent well-paying jobs were available, if there was adequate child care, leave for family responsibilities, and enforced laws on equal employment and pay, a large portion of those counted as outside the labour force would be counted in. The employment statistics give no indication of the number of workers stuck in low-paying, dead-end jobs with no hope for improvement because of a lack of opportunity to upgrade basic literacy and numeracy skills and because of an underinvestment in training by employers and government.

6. Although Canada has a very stable workforce, each year millions of workers experience the turbulence and distress of unemployment and job change. Most leading industrial economies have labour adjustment policies in place to facilitate such transitions and to make the adjustments as painless as possible. Canadian workers have been shortchanged. In Canada, programs that help workers adjust have been under attack for years. The total lack of a full employment commitment, a diminished income support system and the absence of adequate training opportunities have

maximized the damage of change for workers, and, at the same time, has denied access to the workforce for many women, visible minorities, persons with disabilities and Aboriginal Canadians. Clearly, workers have an enormous stake in promoting policies to facilitate labour adjustment.

7. The most important element of adjustment policy and on which every labour policy and social program depends, however, is full employment. It was not until 1945 that the government declared a full employment policy. However, it never went as far as to introduce a Full Employment Act. Nevertheless, full employment was a feature — although not a strong one — of federal economic policy up until the mid-1970s when it was abandoned.

8. Until 1990, the last surviving remnant of the federal commitment to full employment was in the Unemployment Insurance Act. Before Bill C-21, the UI Act obligated government to pay the total cost of extended UI benefits resulting from high unemployment. For each half percentage point that the unemployment rate was above 4 percent, benefits were extended by two weeks for a maximum extension of thirty-two weeks over and above the regular entitlement. With Bill C-21, the Tories repealed this financial liability and effectively removed the only full employment commitment in a federal law.

The Tory/Corporate Adjustment Plan

9. Since its election in 1984, the Mulroney government has set out to wipe UI from the public accounts, but not by reducing unemployment. The labour market programs painstakingly put in place over the past fifty years, such as Unemployment Insurance, are being gutted.

10. After the Forget Commission failed and they were safely re-elected, the Tories, in 1989, introduced Bill C-21 to amend the UI Act. It was much more than a few amendments to UI. It was, as the Tories described it, a labour force development strategy. The strategy was clearly tailored to their corporate agenda. The primary goal was to

redefine the nature and causes of unemployment and the purpose of UI itself. This was done in two ways: by removing the government's obligation for extended UI benefits due to high unemployment, and by attributing unemployment to a lack of worker skills. They began the process of linking training with UI entitlements.

11. Getting rid of the government's $3 billion liability for extended UI benefits was only part of the Tory plan. An even more important objective was to eliminate the explicit legal liability for policy failure and the implied social covenant for unemployment greater than 4 percent. The unemployed, in the Tory global vision, are regarded as unfortunate but necessary casualties. According to the federal employment minister, "The increase in unemployment here is not good for those who have lost their jobs. But if that's what it takes to make Canadian industry more competitive, it is worth it."

12. The Tories want Canadians to believe that unemployment is not the result of their economic policies but a result of poor worker skills, a problem created by workers themselves. The employment minister asserts, "The problem in Canada is not a shortage of jobs, it is a shortage of skills."

13. Because of this strategy, the Tories are not concerned about how the unemployed will pay for the groceries or the rent. Instead of having a full employment strategy, the Tories are using the fear of poverty as a powerful instrument to force workers to adjust to lower wages and accept lower standards of work. Bill C-21 not only cut benefits, but also introduced provisions to give bonuses to unemployed workers who accepted a job, any job, quickly.

14. The government doesn't see its labour force development strategy ending with Bill C-21. It has already started to build a case to make training a condition for UI entitlement. The employment minister explained the government's position this way: "What I'm saying, therefore, is those on welfare who choose not to learn or choose not to improve themselves, they will just make a decision to remain poor all their lives ... And given the magnitude of

the debt that is there, how long can we continue paying people to do just nothing?"

15. Their solution is worker-financed training by the unemployed through cuts in UI benefits and increased UI premiums. By institutionally linking the issue of skills and unemployment through the UI system, the Tories accomplish their financial objective of cutting UI benefits while at the same time justifying their actions to the public by saying that unemployment is caused by workers lacking skills.

16. In this way, the Tories have used one of the most powerful labour adjustment instruments as a means of institutionalizing their economic agenda under the guise of a labour force strategy. It goes well beyond the immediate purpose of justifying massive UI benefit cuts. It victimizes the unemployed and undermines the primary purpose of the UI program, which is to provide income support for the unemployed. This linkage deceitfully defines mass unemployment as a skills and training issue rather than what it really is — a failed economic policy issue.

17. Others, in the media and elsewhere, have bought into the view that unemployment is due to a lack of worker skills and they promote training and retraining as substitutes for income support to the unemployed and job creation measures by the government. It is absurd to suggest that everyone who loses his/her job somehow needs training.

18. The Tory/corporate agenda of "competitiveness" has replaced any commitment to full employment. It has become a wrap for a whole package of other myths: "More training is necessary because we are moving to a high-tech future." "Higher trained technology jobs mean higher wages." "A more highly trained workforce will mean more jobs in Canada and a lack of training has hindered the development of the Canadian economy." These were among the myths used by the federal government to sell the massive cuts to UI benefits and to cancel the government's own insurance contribution for unemployment over 4 percent.

19. The biggest myth of all, however, is the suggestion that the income support of UI can replace government or employer spending on training. The purpose of UI is to provide income to pay for housing, food, clothing and transportation while searching for another job.
20. Employers have every reason to rejoice with the Mulroney strategy. It removes the responsibility from employers for investing in the training of their employees. As it is, three quarters of Canadian companies spend nothing on training their own employees. Total yearly expenditures on training and retraining by the private sector is about $160 per worker, and most of this is for management and sales training. At the same time, they insist the key element to competitiveness is people, not markets, technology, access to raw materials or financial resources. The training record of public sector employers is no better.
21. There is no public pressure on employers to train or retrain their own employees. The Tories have not accepted proposals for an employer-training tax.
22. Instead of introducing policies to force employers to provide training, the Mulroney government has turned billions of federal training dollars over to the private sector. Formerly, these dollars went directly to the public educational institutions. Under the privatization scheme of the Canadian Jobs Strategy (CJS), business can use the money to provide the training itself or purchase the training, either from a community college or from a private trainer. There is no requirement that the skills be portable or meet any prescribed standard. Instead of a training tax on employers, the Tories have provided wage subsidies with virtually no requirements for quality training.
23. On top of this, and despite all of the Tory talk about training, federal spending on training has steadily declined since they were elected in 1984. Until Bill C-21, all federal assistance for training was financed from general government revenues. In 1985, the Tories rolled all federal training dollars into the CJS and promised to spend $2 billion per year. Instead, funding was cut each year. This

year it was cut another $100 million to $1.6 billion. Income support is a much smaller part of CJS funds. In 1992, more federal support for training will come from the UI system than from general government revenues. Under the Tory changes to UI, up to 15 percent ($3 billion) may be spent on training and a whole range of developmental uses of UI.

24. Although most developmental uses of UI this year is to provide income support, it nevertheless would be legal to use all UI developmental use funds for non-income support purposes under Bill C-21. Clearly, the Tory strategy is to fund all training from UI premiums and phase out funding from general government revenues. Under this strategy, UI premiums are a disguised payroll training tax on workers.

25. The government's high unemployment policy has sent UI expenditures skyrocketing to $20 billion. Double digit unemployment, together with the withdrawal of the government payment for extended benefits, have increased UI premiums by 82 percent since 1989, and the deficit on the UI account will be nearly $5 billion by the end of 1992. Revenues from UI premiums are second only to personal income taxes in overall government revenues.

26. The Tory UI training strategy is costing workers dearly. The greatest cost, of course, is borne by the unemployed. In 1992, over a million and a half unemployed will lose benefits because of Bill C-21 changes. The biggest losers will be the hundreds of thousands who will not even qualify for UI Over a million of those who do qualify will exhaust their claim before finding another job. The loss in benefits to the unemployed in 1992 will be about $3 billion, but it doesn't end there.

27. The Tories have restructured the system to force further huge cuts in benefits. The implications for premium payers and beneficiaries alike are clear. They are positioning the UI system to fail as an income support program. The Tory/corporate "competitive" agenda is to have high unemployment to force and keep wages down. Yet employers complain that the cost of UI premiums is unsupportable if

all the program does is provide income support for the unemployed.
28. The pressure is steadily mounting to make UI benefits conditional upon training. Yet the Tory/corporate connection has been silent on "training for what jobs."

Labour's Adjustment Policies

29. Labour's vision of programs to help workers adjust or change jobs is obviously very different. To be successful, adjustment programs must go hand in hand with policies that promote full employment.
30. In the absence of a full employment policy, any set of labour adjustment measures, no matter how cleverly put together, are doomed to fail. The Tories describe their policy of training the unemployed as an "active" labour market policy, but training is not a substitute for full employment nor does training create jobs. Training is also not a substitute for earnings replacement provided by UI.
31. In Sweden, where active labour market policies were pioneered, "active" has quite a different meaning. Active means policies that avoid unemployment. It means programs to assist workers entering the labour force or workers threatened by closure. The assistance — including training — is provided before layoff. It means requiring employers to provide adequate notice of layoff. Pro-active measures make training more effective and the transition to a new job much less painful and costly.
32. Labour's policy on worker adjustment stands on five pillars: First, active government measures are needed to create jobs. Second, there must be income support for workers who lose their jobs. Third, workers must be equipped with the necessary education and training. Fourth, there must be legislation put in place to govern layoffs and plant closures and improved labour standards which remove barriers to employment. Fifth, there must be a national employment service accessible to every worker providing comprehensive information on job vacancies,

counselling, job placement, unemployment insurance and assistance programs.

33. First and foremost, active government measures are needed to create jobs. Jobs are created by economic policies that maintain or stimulate demand, thereby increasing the production of goods and services. Government also needs to directly stimulate the economy through major new investments to meet the needs of people. The government has an important role in job creation via the public sector. Not only are these jobs well paid and unionized, they contribute to a valuable economic and social infrastructure which benefits both individuals and business.

34. Unemployment is, in fact, the measure of government policy failure. Unemployment is the result of federal economic policies that reduce the demand for our goods and services at home and abroad. Free trade, high interest rates, the high dollar, privatization, deregulation, massive cuts in government spending, tax measures like the GST and numerous other policies have created the continuing unemployment crisis.

35. The underlying assumption of all labour adjustment policy is full employment. Labour market policies are intended to deal with the transitions the working age population go through. They assume you are in a job, moving out of a job, or moving into a job. The issue then is how best to protect people while they are either employed, unemployed or not in the labour force.

36. The Canadian Labour Congress will continue to be a strong defender of our UI system. If the UI system is to survive, labour must work to have the key features of the Tory changes reversed.

37. The government must pay for extended benefits when the unemployment rate is above 4 percent. It is the government's liability for unemployment created by its own policies. We insist that the developmental use of UI be restricted to income support and we will continue to oppose the use of UI premiums to finance the purchase of

training courses and other non-income support uses of UI.

38. There are very important historical, constitutional and labour market reasons for viewing UI as a much broader instrument of labour market policy, but not in the way fashioned by the Tories. For example, the UI Act could be used as a very effective instrument in regulating permanent layoffs and workplace closures.

39. The 1971 reforms to the UI Act went well beyond insuring the interruption of earnings for more reasons than layoff or job loss. As an earnings insurance plan, it was broadened to include maternity leave, sickness and voluntary quits. They also linked the risk of unemployment to the failure of government policy to achieve full employment. These principles must be maintained.

40. With lifelong learning now an integral part of working life it is necessary to look at new approaches to insuring the interruption of earnings against various possible contingencies. Clearly, UI should be used to provide income support to unemployed workers to take training to reenter the paid workforce.

Training

41. Training is an essential element of a full employment strategy but training cannot substitute for full employment because training does not create jobs.

42. The Canadian labour movement has a long history in promoting government policy on skills training. At the turn of the century, the Canadian Trades and Labour Congress asked the federal government to become more involved in vocational training. The first government involvement in Canada came in 1910 with the appointment of a federal Royal Commission on Industrial Training and Technical Education.

43. Labour adjustment programs began to emerge in Canada as early as 1919 following the First World War. Fearing social and political unrest from mass unemployment with the return of the troops, the federal government financed a

national network of employment offices to help youth find jobs and passed the country's first training legislation: the Technical Education Act.

44. Although training is a shared jurisdiction with the provinces, the federal government historically has provided the leadership. The provinces viewed training more in the realm of economic policy. It is relatively recent that education, in the broadest sense, was viewed as economic.

45. But our influence on federal training policy has not been what it should be. Workers have an enormous stake in the shaping of training policy.

46. Labour believes training is a right. The right must be universal. It must be available without barriers to all employed workers, the unemployed and the working age population wanting to enter or reenter the labour force. This right must be entrenched in employment law. Every worker should be entitled to a minimum of forty hours of training each year during normal working hours without a loss of pay.

47. Training must be seen as a fundamental part of the job. Labour has long advocated a levy/grant or training tax on employers for training. Employers who provide approved training to their employees would receive compensation from the training fund.

48. Training for the unemployed and people wishing to enter or reenter the labour force should be funded out of general revenue. There should be an income support program for those ineligible for UI. Social support services also must be provided.

49. Training rights include paid educational leave. Adult workers who have not completed high school should be entitled to paid leave.

50. The content of training must be geared to workers' needs as they see them and must be developmental. Skills must be taught in a way that goes beyond a particular job and leaves trainees better able to take on different tasks in the future.

51. Training must equip workers to have more control over technology, their jobs and their work lives, by building on workers' existing capabilities and preparing them for the future. More than just occupational skills are needed in order to eliminate job discrimination based on gender, race or ethnicity.

52. Discrimination has been a feature of workplace-related training. Programs leading to the best jobs have been the preserve of white men. Job-skills training must be structured to correct the exclusion of women, visible minorities and persons with disabilities. To this end, it is essential that we have a universally accessible system of child care.

53. Women attempting to reenter the paid labour force are usually slotted into low paying, less skilled jobs. Other barriers facing women must be dealt with: lack of information about training opportunities, lack of adequate income support, little opportunity to update basic educational skills, spousal opposition, and the lack of job opportunities following training.

54. The pattern of discrimination against visible minorities is maintained by many of the same barriers, compounded by a pattern of institutionalized racism which closes doors to good education and training programs and blocks access to good jobs even when access to training is gained. Every training program must measure its design in terms of how it proposes to overcome hurdles to fairness and equality.

55. Training only makes sense when it is part of an economic strategy for full employment, for the creation of good paying secure jobs and for a labour process which relies on workers' skills rather than one which dismisses skills and the workers.

56.[*] The trade union movement has fought for many years for an educational system that is open to everyone so that they can gain the skills and knowledge to function fully in their lives at work, at home and in the community. Training programs must be carried out in conjunction with public

---

* See 1992 Amendment on page 122.

educational institutions. Some of these institutions may have to modify their own structures and approaches, but they are an invaluable resource suited to channeling training in a broader direction, sensitive to the needs of workers as clients and offering accountability to the public.

57. All Canadians have a right to a good basic education. Opportunities to upgrade literacy and numeracy skills are an essential part of the training process.

Apprenticeship Reform

58. Apprenticeship training accounts for less than 10 percent of total trainees. Of the 270 apprenticeable occupations in Canada, nearly half of all Canadian apprentices are in a half dozen trades like carpentry, auto mechanics, and electrical. The system is in urgent need of reform.

59. With generous federal assistance (including capital assistance) for institutional training, enrolment in community colleges increased by about 300 percent in the 1960s, compared to 30 percent for apprenticeship.

60. There are many reasons for the relative decline in apprenticeship: the shared jurisdiction for training between the federal government and provinces, the hostility of employers to trades because of their higher wages and power over the organization of work, and the "bookish" bias of the educational establishment.

61. In apprenticeship, employment, teaching and learning are linked. Apprenticeship training essentially combines the elements of employed worker training and new entrant training. It is as relevant to the emerging occupations of a post-industrial economy as it was in the past. These unique aspects must guide its operation.

62. The current "time-based" programs which allow the apprentice to learn from the journeyperson must not be replaced by a system that assumes that the required skills can be identified, listed and tested outside of the workplace. There is no substitute for experience which only comes with time and practice on the job.

63. The in-school portion of training must continue to be interspersed with practical experience in the workplace. The education system should not be used simply as a screening device before employers make a commitment.
64. Apprenticeship training must become accessible to all. This will require better efforts to acquaint guidance counsellors and other youth advisors with information about apprenticeship training. It will also require new programs to target women and visible minority employees as potential apprentices with their current employers.

New Structures And New Relationships

65. Workers have an advisory as well as a decision-making role in adjustment programs. This principle has been an accepted feature of public policy for over fifty years, beginning with the establishment of the Unemployment Insurance Commission in which there was an equal number of commissioners representing workers and employers. The advisory councils for labour market programs at the national level have generally followed this principle. It was followed with the establishment of the Canadian Labour Force Development Board (CLFDB).
66. These principles have not been applied in the appointments to the several hundred federal committees and councils at the local and sectoral level. Labour had virtually no representation on local advisory councils and community futures committees under the CJS. Workers have only a token number of representatives on sectoral committees.
67. Workers and their unions must play a central role in determining, at all levels, the direction of training. The principles we have adopted for decision-making structures at the national, provincial, local and sectoral levels, must become even more firmly rooted in public policy. This requires labour/business parity on all training and adjustment boards, committees and councils; co-chairing of boards; representatives from equity groups and education should not exceed one third of board membership; and

boards should have executive powers as well as an advisory role. The CLC will name labour representatives at the national level. The provincial federations of labour in consultations with the local councils will appoint labour representatives to local labour force boards.

68. The mandate and appointment process for the national board (CLFDB) and other boards that will be established at the provincial/territorial and local levels is not yet in legislation. Labour will insist that both the mandate and stakeholder representation be defined in federal and provincial legislation.

69. Business continues to dominate the governing and advisory boards of community colleges and vocational institutions. To correct this, governance of these institutions must be turned over to boards that genuinely represent the diverse interests of labour, business, and other groups within the community including teachers, support staff and students. Each board must be composed of external and internal members. One third of external board members must represent labour. There should be an equal number representing business and an equal number representing the community in its diversity. Board members should be reimbursed for expenses and lost wages for board business.

70. Training for employed workers should be funded by a new training tax on employers. The programs funded by this tax should be approved by the CLFDB. In France, by law, each company has to invest 1.3 percent of its salary base in training and retraining. Large companies spend considerably more, bringing the national average to 2.5 percent of gross salary. This is five times the Canadian expenditure.

71. Up until the 1960s, a very large percentage of job placements were through the National Employment Service. The service now accounts for a mere fraction of total job placements. The system is handicapped by lack of comprehensive job vacancy information. Job counselling without any information on available jobs may do more harm than good. This can demoralize, frustrate and mislead the

APPENDIX II

worker into a hopeless search.

72. A key requirement of the UI system is that the claimant undertake an intensive job search to maintain the claim and receive benefits. It is a feature we strongly support. Without comprehensive information on local or rational job openings, however, the job search requirement becomes a farce.

73. Many countries with pro-active or active labour market policies, such as Sweden and Germany, require employers to register all job openings with their National Employment Service. Canada is one of the few advanced industrial nations that does not gather job vacancy information from employers.

74. Not only is there no requirement that employers register job vacancies, there is not even a monthly survey done by Statistics Canada. Such a survey would be helpful in planning for skill needs, but it is no substitute for a registry of job vacancies. Job information is an absolute essential for employed and unemployed workers alike. It should be mandatory to register all job vacancies with the Canada Employment and Immigration Commission.

75. Even when jobs are available, the lack of information is not the only problem. Thousands of workers are forced to turn to unregulated private placement agencies. Other than a municipal business licence, private placement agencies have no restrictions or conditions on their operations. For example, there are no requirements that they inform workers of basic minimum employment standards or worker entitlements. These agencies must be both limited and strictly regulated.

76. Canadians must have access to a one-stop national employment service which includes counselling, job placement, job vacancy information, financial assistance and UI administration. It must be available in every community across the country. The Tories have seriously weakened the National Employment Service and allowed absolutely vital functions such as the "labour market exchange" to die.

77. The federal government has consistently eroded the services available to the workforce through its policies of cutbacks and privatization. The national network of Canada Employment Centres must be strengthened and provided with the necessary resources to expand publicly administered employment services.

Advancing Labour's Policies

78. The CLC will continue its campaign to force the government to amend the UI Act, to restore benefits to their pre-Bill C-21 level, and to restore the government's payment of extended benefits when the unemployment rate is above 4 percent.

79. The Congress will also work to have the developmental use of UI provisions of the UI Act restricted to income support, and we will continue to oppose the use of worker UI premiums to finance the purchase of training courses and other non-income support uses of UI.

80. The CLC and its affiliates will campaign for the repeal of the regulation requiring severance and pension income to be treated as earnings for the purpose of receiving UI benefits.

81. The Congress will press for federal legislation which will require one year's advance notice for workplace closures and six months notice for permanent layoff.

82. The CLC will press for an amendment to the UI Act which would make the creation of worker/employer adjustment committees mandatory in the event of a closure or mass layoff.

83.* The CLC, its affiliates and federations of labour will work to ensure the implementation of labour's training policy as outlined in this paper and which includes the following elements:

   a) training is a right which must be entrenched in legislation;

---

* See 1992 Amendment on page 122.

b) a minimum of forty hours of training each year during normal working hours without loss of pay;

c) paid educational leave;

d) an end to discrimination which has been a feature of workplace related training — training must be accessible to all;

e) a new employer-training tax to fund training for employed workers;

f) income support while on training for the unemployed who are not UI claimants to be funded out of general revenue;

g) access to literacy and numeracy upgrading; and

h)* training to be delivered in conjunction with public education institutions.

84.* The CLC will pressure the federal government to expand its employment service into a comprehensive, one-stop service which meets the varied needs of both unemployed and employed workers. Further, we will demand that these services be delivered through the public sector.

85.* To assist workers seeking employment, the Congress will press the federal government to provide a registry of job vacancies.

86.* As a condition for its participation, the Congress, its affiliates and federation of labour will continue to insist on labour/business parity on all training and adjustment boards, committees and councils. Labour will continue to press governments to define in legislation both the mandate of and representation on these boards.

---

* See 1992 Amendment on page 122.

Amendment to the Training and Unemployment Insurance Policy Statement

19th Constitutional Convention
June 18th to June 12th, 1992

WE CAN DO IT: INVEST IN TRAINING AND RESTORE U.I.

1. Begin paragraph 56 with a new sentence:
   We are opposed to private for-profit training.

2. New 83. The CLC recognizes the legitimacy of existing union controlled training programs.

3. Number 83 becomes number 84; and delete point h).

4. New 85. The CLC, its affiliates, federations and labour councils will work to ensure that:

   a) public institutions continue to be the primary deliverers of training;
   b) funds be made available to ensure the continuing strength of public education institutions; and
   c) public institutions remain the preferred means of training.

5. Number 84 becomes number 86.

6. Number 85 becomes number 87.

7. Number 86 becomes number 88.

Appendix III

Canadian Autoworkers (CAW)

MASTER AGREEMENT BETWEEN GENERAL MOTORS OF CANADA LIMITED AND THE CAW

dated October 11, 1990
(Effective: October 15, 1990)

Attachment to Letter

A TUITION REFUND PLAN FOR GENERAL MOTORS HOURLY-RATE EMPLOYEES

General Motors of Canada Limited, as a part of its continuing effort to encourage employee development, established a Tuition Refund Plan for its hourly-rate employees in 1964. The purpose of the Plan is to provide financial assistance to an eligible employee who desires to further personal training and education through spare time, job-related or basic education courses. This Plan was changed in 1968 and has been revised again through the joint efforts of General Motors and the Union.

Eligibility

It is recognized that certain eligibility provisions must be established to provide for fair and equitable administration of the Plan. Therefore, an employee to be eligible to participate in the Plan and receive a tuition refund payment must have seniority during the entire period of a course of study and be in active service at the beginning of the course for which tuition is to be refunded except as otherwise specified in the letter to which this attachment is appended concerning an employee laid off as a result of a Plant Closing who, at the time of such layoff, had five (5) or more years of seniority. Employees not considered eligible for this program are: probationary employees, students dividing their time between studies in a recognized educational institution and work in a Company plant or office, and employees on educational leaves of absence or leaves of absence for union activity, or for public office.

Further, an employee must obtain Company approval prior to undertaking a course for refund. In order to receive a refund, the employee will provide evidence that the course was completed on a basis satisfactory to the Company (ie, a passing grade or other satisfactory evidence of completion). Also, the employee will present evidence of payment and the amount of such payment for the course completed.

Tuition Refund

An eligible employee will receive a refund of the full amount of the tuition and compulsory fees for an approved course or courses up to a maximum of *$1,000* during the calendar year (*$1,500* for the calendar year for approved courses taken at an accredited college or university). Such costs for approved courses will be refunded under the Plan upon satisfactory completion of each course, term or semester. If an employee is not in active service at such time, payment will be made provided the employee has seniority recall rights. Application of the applicable maximum amount of eligibility will relate to the calendar year of completion of the approved course or courses and not to the calendar year in which the refund is approved.

Although the Plan reimburses an employee for tuition and compulsory fees, no reimbursement will be made for the cost of books, transportation or any other expenses. Participants whose tuition is covered by benefits resulting from government aid, or scholarship aid will be eligible for a refund only for that portion of the tuition and compulsory fees not covered by such benefits.

Courses

Courses to be approved under the Plan will include those related to maintaining and improving the employee's skill in performing the employee's job or contributing to such employee's general development within the Company. The following programs are considered job-related and will be approved when the needs cannot be met within the Company:

- Courses which will improve the employee's skill on such employee's present job. This includes courses designed to update employees in the technology of their trade or occupation;
- Courses which relate to the next job in the logical development of an employee's career;
- Courses which will prepare an employee for openings that are expected to occur in the future and for which a sufficient number of qualified employees are not available;
- Courses taken to complete the requirements for a grammar school certificate or high school diploma;
- Any literacy courses or courses in fundamental reading and mathematics. These include courses usually designed to teach sixth grade competency in reading, writing and numerical skills;
- Any required or pertinent elective courses taken in a degree-seeking program in a field related to the employee's job or

appropriate to the employee's career in General Motors;
- Courses of instruction in approved educational or training institutions directed toward qualifying an employee as an apprentice in the skilled trades.

Correspondence Courses

The Tuition Refund Plan is intended to cover courses taken at approved local institutions, and correspondence courses are not included under its general provisions. Under exceptional circumstances, correspondence courses offered by well-recognized institutions may be approved but only if comparable instruction is not available locally.

Institutions

Courses approved for tuition refund will be limited to those institutions listed in the current directory of the Association of Universities and Colleges of Canada; any recognized secondary school; and such other local institutions approved by Management which provide equivalent instructions.

Time Required for School Attendance and Study

Employees studying under the Tuition Refund Plan will be expected to complete the requirements of school attendance and homework assignments in hours outside their scheduled hours of work. It is not expected that such employees will receive special consideration in job assignments or work schedules by reasons of participation in this program. However, inability to complete a course once undertaken because of job requirements, may be considered warranting a tuition refund.

Administration

The Company shall be responsible for the interpretation and

general administration of the Plan. An employee having a question regarding interpretation or administration may take it up with the employee's plant or operation. No such question, however, shall be subject to the arbitration procedure of union agreements. Although a standard GM application form is available, local procedures may be established to cover approvals required and other details of administration.

MASTER AGREEMENT BETWEEN GENERAL MOTORS OF CANADA LIMITED AND THE CAW

dated October 11, 1990
Doc. No. 104

CAW LEADERSHIP TRAINING PROGRAM

During current negotiations the parties have discussed the labour education program developed by the Union for the purpose of upgrading the skills which employees utilize in all aspects of trade union functions and the matter of Company financial support of this program. This program, currently known as the CAW Leadership Training Program (P.E.L. Trust), has received contributions from the Company *since* March of 1980.

In recognition, therefore, of the contributions this program can make to the improvement of the Union/Management relationship and toward more effective administration of the Collective Agreement, the Company agrees as hereinafter set forth to making a grant to the CAW Leadership Training Program (P.E.L. Trust), herein called the "P.E.L. Trust."

An educational leave of absence for participation in the Union's Leadership Training Program will be granted by the Company in accordance with the provisions of the Master Agreement to seniority employees designed by the President National Union CAW on four (4) weeks' advance written notice to the Direction of Labour Relations for the Company specifying the employee's name and dates of requested absence, provided no such absence will result in any loss of efficiency or disruption of operations at the Company's plants.

Employees granted such leaves will be excused from work without pay for up to twenty (20) days of class time, plus travel time where necessary, said leaves of absence to be intermittent over a twelve (12) month period from the first day of leave during the term of the *current* Agreement.

AGREEMENT BETWEEN DEHAVILLAND AIRCRAFT CO. OF CANADA A DIVISION OF BOEING OF CANADA LTD. AND CAW LOCAL 112

June 23, 1990

Training Representative

9.06

(a) The Company will recognize a full time Training Representative to assist in the co-ordination of the training programs agreed to by the parties. The Training Representative shall be allowed free access to and from the Company's Operations in the performance of his duties. He will be provided with a desk and a chair in the Plant Chairman's office.

(b) The Training Representative shall receive the rate of equal pay to the rate for the job classification which he held upon election or appointment as the Training Representative and will be paid the equivalent of forty (40) hours per week at straight time.

(c) When the Training Representative ceases to hold office, he shall be returned, consistent with his seniority to the classification and to the department in which he was employed at the time of his election or appointment as Training Representative, or to a job classification embracing comparable job duties to that which he held prior to his election or appointment.

MASTER AGREEMENT BETWEEN CHRYSLER CANADA LTD. AND THE CAW

October 25, 1990

PRODUCTION AND MAINTENANCE

(Excerpts)

New Technology (71)

There shall be established a Skilled Trades Committee on New Technology, made up of 2 skilled tradespersons from the Union and 2 Company Representatives.

•••

Both parties agree that skilled trades employees should be afforded the opportunity to receive the training required to service any new technology machinery or equipment being introduced to the production process.

This training will be made available through short-range specialized programs deemed necessary to implement this new technology where it is agreed that such work falls within the scope of the bargaining unit.

The method of providing this training will be discussed with the committee and due consideration will be given to seniority when selecting employees to be trained.

•••

New Technology (64)

The Corporation and the Union may submit to the National Training Committee their recommendations for any training programs intended to assist present employees to perform work within the bargaining unit which is new or changed as a result of technological improvement.

MASTER AGREEMENT BETWEEN A. G. SIMPSON AND THE CAW

September 9, 1992

Adjustment

42.02

Adjustment Program to be effective in cases of complete or partial plant closures as defined in Article 42.01 above:

(a) The Company will participate in a labour-management adjustment committee and that we will seek financial assistance from the Industrial Adjustment Service (federal government) and the Office of Labour Adjustment (in Ontario).

(b) Every worker who is to be laid off will receive an in-depth (one hour) individual needs assessment conducted on Company time, and provided at Company expense.

(c) The Bargaining Committee and the Union Representatives on the Adjustment Committee will be provided four (4) days of training on adjustment issues and processes as determined by the Bargaining Committee. The training will be conducted on Company time and at Company expense.

(d) The Company will provide adequate release time to members of the Adjustment Committee to effectively do their jobs.

(e) Office space for an Action Centre equipped with computers, telephones and other office machinery, will be provided by the Company.

APPENDIX III

(f) Release time will be provided for a full-time Union Coordinator to staff the Action Centre, as well as the required secretarial support, or a maximum period of three months except in the event of a full plant closure, in which case such period of time will be worked out by mutual agreement.

(g) Release time will be granted and tuition costs covered for basic upgrading courses such as English, Math, Computer Awareness, and Blueprint Reading. Such training to be determined by the Adjustment Committee on the basis of the needs assessment and to be provided on Company time to a maximum of forty (40) hours per employer affected.

Appendix IV

Ontario Public Service Employees Union

"SAMPLE CLAUSES ON TRAINING" IN COMMUNITY COLLEGES (CAAT)

SUPPORT STAFF

1. **WORK RELATED – TUITION REIMBURSED**

   9.2 Maintenance of Salary
   An employee absent from work during regular working hours for the purposes of attending courses directly or indirectly related to his/her work and in which the College has directed or approved his/her participation shall not suffer any loss of pay with respect to his/her regular straight time hourly earnings during the period of any such absences.

APPENDIX IV

2. NON-WORK RELATED – TUITION REIMBURSED

9.1 Reimbursement for Tuition
Employees who successfully complete educational courses with the prior approval of the College, either at the College or another educational setting, will be reimbursed by the College for all or part of the tuition fees paid by the employee.

3. FAMILIARIZATION IN JOB POSTING

15.4.7 Familiarization Period
Where the term "fully qualified to perform the work without training" is used in this Article, it is understood that the College shall provide the employees selected with a reasonable period of familiarization, where necessary.

4. JOB SECURITY – PRE-LAYOFF

15.3.4 Recommendations
It shall be the duty of the Committee to consider the matter and to make recommendations to the President of the College with respect to any or all of the alternatives listed below which might be resorted to in order to prevent or minimize the dislocation of employees:

1. Potential creation of vacancies that might be filled by affected employees;
2. Conversion of part-time positions and/or displacement of non-bargaining unit employees;
3. The utilization of other means, such as normal retirements, voluntary leaves or transfers in order to prevent or minimize the effects of the action contemplated;
4. The improvement of employment potential for employees affected by the provision of training or retraining programs and job counselling;
5. Investigation of potential alternative job opportunities that might exist for employees affected both within and outside the College, such as comparable employment opportunities.

It will be the duty of the Committee to make recommendations to the President of the College within ten (10) working days of the establishment of the Committee. Where the Committee is unable to agree on any recommendations, the members appointed by the Union and the members appointed by the College may make separate recommendations. Where separate recommendations are to be delivered they will be exchanged between the appointees prior to delivery.

5. JOB SECURITY RELATED – POST-LAYOFF

15.7 Retraining

15.7.1 Tuition Fee
Where a person who was in the Bargaining Unit has been laid off by the College, pursuant to the provisions of Article 15, the College agrees to provide for a nominal tuition fee of not more than twenty (20) dollars per course:

1. credit courses; or,
2. other courses as are mutually agreed,

which the College offers. The employee must meet the College entrance and admission requirements and is subject to academic policies.

15.7.2 Duration of Retraining
This retraining opportunity shall continue for up to three (3) years from the date of layoff or until such person is recalled, whichever occurs first. Where a person has not completed a course or program in which he/she is enrolled at the time of recall, the College shall consider ways of enabling the individual to complete the course or program.

15.7.3 Re-employment Assistance
The College agrees to assist persons laid off from the Bargaining Unit towards achieving re-employment by providing career counselling, job search assistance, and

APPENDIX IV

retraining opportunities through the application of existing College services.

15.7.4 Consideration for Employment in Non-Bargaining Unit Work

In addition to the recall rights contained in Article 15.6, a person on layoff with in excess of five (5) years' seniority who is participating in retraining pursuant to Article 15.7, of a full time nature, may make a written request to the College's Human Resource Department for consideration for employment in non-bargaining unit work during his/her non-study period. The College shall make an effort to assist him/her in locating suitable non-bargaining unit work within the College.

15.8 Contracting Out – Union Notification

If the College decides to contract out work or services which are being performed by employees at the commencement date of this Agreement which would cause the layoff or involuntary displacement of any employees covered by this Agreement, the College will notify the Union four (4) weeks in advance of the written notice being provided to the employees affected. The processes in Article 15.3 shall be followed.

"SAMPLE CLAUSES ON TRAINING" IN COMMUNITY COLLEGES (CAAT)

CAAT ACADEMIC

1. PROFESSIONAL DEVELOPMENT

4.01 (8) (a) The College shall allow each teacher at least ten (10) working days of professional development in each academic year.

4.01 (8) (b) Unless otherwise agreed between the teacher and the supervisor, the allowance of ten (10) days shall include one period of at least five (5) consecutive working days for professional development.

4.01 (8) (c) The arrangements for such professional development shall be made following discussion between the supervisor and the teacher subject to agreement between the supervisor and the teacher, and such agreement shall not be unreasonably withheld.

4.04 (2) (a) The College shall allow each Counsellor and Librarian at least ten (10) working days of professional development in each academic year.

4.04 (2) (b) Unless otherwise agreed between the Counsellor or Librarian and the supervisor, the allowance of ten (10) days shall include one period of at least five (5) consecutive working days for professional development.

4.04 (2) (c) The arrangements for such professional development shall be made following discussion between the supervisor and the Counsellor or Librarian subject to agreement between the supervisor and the Counsellor or Librarian, and such agreement shall not be unreasonably withheld.

4.08 In keeping with the professional responsibility of the teacher, non-teaching periods are used for activities initiated by the teacher and by the College as part of the parties' mutual commitment to professionalism, the quality of education and professional development.

Such activities will be undertaken by mutual consent and agreement will not be unreasonably withheld.

Such activities will neither be recorded nor scheduled except as in accordance with Article 4.01(7) (a).

2. PROFESSIONAL DEVELOPMENT LEAVE (SABBATICAL)

18.01 The College recognizes that it is in the interests of employees, students and the College that employees are given the opportunity by the College to pursue College-approved professional development activities outside the College through further academic or technical studies or in industry where such activities will enhance the ability of the employee upon return to the College to fulfill professional responsibilities.

18.02 To that end, each College will grant a minimum of two (2) percent of full-time members of the academic bargaining unit of the College concerned who have been members of the bargaining unit for a period of not less than six (6) years, and an additional one (1) percent of full-time members of the academic bargaining unit for a period of not less than fifteen (15) years, to be absent on professional development leave at any one time in accordance with the following conditions:

(a) the purpose of the leave is for College-approved academic, technical, industrial or other pursuits where such activities will enhance the ability of the teacher, counsellor or librarian upon return to the College;
(b) a suitable substitute can be obtained;
(c) the leave will normally be for a period of from one (1) to twelve (12) months;
(d) the employee, upon termination of the professional development leave, will return to the College granting the leave for a period of at least one (1) year, failing which the employee shall repay the College all salaries and fringe benefits received by the employee while on professional development leave;
(e) the salary paid to the employee will be based on the following scale; fifty-five percent (55%) of the employee's normal salary increasing by five percent (5%) per year after six (6) years of employment with the College concerned to a maximum of seventy percent (70%) of the employee's normal salary after nine (9) years. It is understood that the College's payment is subject to reduction if the aggregate of the College's payment and compensation or payments from other sources during the period exceeds the amount of the employee's normal salary. The amount and condi-

tions of payment will be pro-rated for shorter leaves;
(f) applications for professional development leave will be submitted in writing containing a detailed statement of the nature of the proposed leave and its perceived benefit to the College and the employee; to the Chair of the Department at least six (6) months prior to the commencement date;
(g) all applicants will be notified in writing by the President as to the disposition of their application for professional development leave;
(h) the College may on its own initiative propose plans of professional development leave to employees; however no employee shall be under obligation to accept such a proposal;
(i) the provisions of the Article shall not preclude the College from permitting greater numbers of employees to be absent on professional development leave;
(j) the fulfillment of the minimum of two percent (2%) of full-time employees on professional development leave (arising out of employee-initiated leaves) as set out herein will depend upon the receipt and approval by the College of a sufficient number of qualified applications in accordance with the criteria set out above;
(k) in the event that more eligible employees apply for professional development leave than will be approved, preference shall be given to the applicants with greater length of service since their last professional development or sabbatical leave under Article 18 of the preceding collective agreements;
(l) an applicant who is denied professional development leave shall be notified in writing of the reasons for the denial. Approval of an application for professional development leave shall not be unreasonably withheld;
(m) for professional development leaves that are granted for a period of less than one (1) year, the payment shall be pro-rated. The unused portion of the allowable earned leave shall be available to the processes of the College and those defined within this article.

Payment for the unused portions of leave when taken shall be paid at the same proportion of salary as established in Article 18.01 (e) when the first portion was taken.

3. IN-SERVICE TRAINING PROGRAM

Council of Regents
for Colleges of
Applied Arts and
Technology

10th Floor
790 Bay Street
Toronto, Ontario
M5G 1N8

Re: Access to the Salary Scale Maximum

The parties reaffirm their on-going commitment to the quality of teaching in the CAAT system. The parties have agreed to the establishment of an In-Service Teacher Training Certificate Program in a modularized format which provides accessibility to the employees at each college. The program is being offered by Confederation College as host institution, and an agreement has been entered into by the Council, OPSEU and the host institution in that regard.

The objectives, curriculum delivery and length of the program will be developed by the task force (established under the previous Collective Agreement), and shall have regard for the accrued experience of CAAT teachers including teacher training courses and programs completed.

Employees who have fifteen (15) years or more of service and whose maximum Step is currently below Step 16 and who enroll and participate in the program shall receive (once only) an immediate one (1) step salary progression, to a maximum of Step 16, and shall maintain that Step upon maintaining satisfactory performance in the program.

Employees who successfully complete the program shall be entitled to progress to Step 16.

J. Clancy
President
Ontario Public Service
Employees Union

C.E. Pascal
Chair
Ontario Council
of Regents

4. TUITION – REDUCED COURSES

18.03 An employee in the bargaining unit may take, for a tuition fee of not more than $20.00, on the employee's own time,

(a) Ministry approved programs or courses, or
(b) other programs or courses as mutually agreed, which the College currently offers. The employee must meet the normal entrance and admission requirements.

5. JOB SECURITY: RETIRING IN BUMPING

8.18 To assist persons who are laid off, the College agrees to the following:

(a) Such a person may take, tuition-free, one (1) program or course offered by the College, for which the person meets the normal entrance and admission requirements. In addition, the College shall consider and implement such retraining opportunities as the College may consider feasible.
(b) Before the College hires a sessional employee, a person who has been laid off under 8.05 within the past twenty-four (24) months and has not elected severance under 8.16 (a) shall be offered the sessional appointment provided that the former employee has the competence, skill, and experience to fulfill the requirements of the sessional position concerned. The applicable salary for the duration of the sessional appointment shall be at the current salary rate, at the step level in effect at the time of lay-off.

For the purposes of Appendix III, the former employee will be deemed to be a new hire. This sessional employee will terminate employment at the end of the sessional appointment.

For the purposes of 8.06 (a) and 8.10 the former employee will be deemed to be still on lay-off during the sessional appointment.

(c) The College shall consider additional means of support such as career counselling and job search assistance where such activities are expected to assist the individual in making the transition to a new career outside the Bargaining Unit.

6. JOB SECURITY – POST-LAYOFF RETIREMENT

(h) (iii) failing placement under paragraph (h) (i) above, such employee shall be laid off with written notice of not less than ninety (90) calendar days. Such employee shall be granted release from all or part of the normally assigned duties, for this period of notice, for the purpose of engaging in retraining activities, where such release is feasible given the normal operational requirements facing the College. Where such release is not possible, the notice period shall be extended by up to ninety (90) days to permit retraining and the employee shall maintain current salary and benefits for the duration of the notice period.

(h) (iv) at the termination of the period referred to in paragraph 8.05 (h) (iii) above, such employee shall be reassigned within the College to a vacant full-time position, if the employee has the competence, skill, and experience to perform the requirements of a vacant full-time position.

(h) (v) failing placement under 8.05 (h) (iv) above, such employee shall be laid off without further notice.

7. JOB SECURITY: EMPLOYMENT STABILITY

28.01 (a) The parties hereto subscribe to certain objectives and principles as follows:

(i) that employment stability should be enhanced, within the resources available, through both long-term and short-term strategies;

(ii) that such strategies could include, but not necessarily be restricted to, planning, retraining, early retirement, alternative assignments, secondments, employee career counselling, job sharing and professional development;
(iii) that data which is relevant to employment stability should be made available to both parties;
(iv) that procedures should be in place to deal with situations that arise in which, notwithstanding the best efforts of both parties, lay-offs and/or reductions in the number of employees who have completed the probationary period become necessary; and,
(v) that resources should be made available to achieve, to the degree that it is feasible, these objectives and principles.

28.01 (b) The parties have agreed to the following provisions, in order to achieve, to the degree that it is feasible, the foregoing objectives and principles.

28.02 (a) There shall be established, at each College, a College Employment Stability Committee (CESC).

28.02 (b) Each CESC will be composed of four (4) members, with two (2) to be appointed by the College and two (2) by the Union Local. The term of office of each member shall be one (1) year, which may be renewable, commencing on September 1 of each year. Alternative arrangements may be made at the local level upon agreement of the Union Local and the College.

28.03 The functions of the CESC shall be to recommend long-term and short-term strategies to enhance employment stability, and to administer and make decisions with respect to the Joint Employment Stability Reserve Fund (JESRF) established under 28.08, as specifically prescribed in 28.04, 28.05 and 28.06.

28.04 The functions of the CESC shall include the making of recommendations with respect to long-term strategies to enhance employment stability, having regard to available resources. Activities may include, but not necessarily be restricted to:

(i) receiving and analyzing data provided under the Collective Agreement with the objective of creating a shared data base;
(ii) identifying needs for further data collection;
(iii) analyzing, on an ongoing basis, internal and external trends which may have impact on employment stability, such as areas of growth and decline and changing resource levels and priorities;
(iv) developing strategies including retraining, early retirement, alternate assignments, secondments, professional leaves, employee career counselling, job sharing, professional development, pre-retirement planning and voluntary transfer.

28.05 (a) The functions of the CESC shall include the making of recommendations with respect to short-term strategies to enhance employment stability, having regard to available resources. Activities may include, but not necessarily be restricted to:

(i) receiving data concerning vacancies at other Colleges under Article 8.12, and distributing information concerning such vacancies and providing assistance to employees regarding such vacancies;
(ii) developing strategies including retraining, early retirement, alternate assignments, secondments, professional leaves, employee career counselling, job sharing, professional development, pre-retirement planning and voluntary transfer;
(iii) identifying local adaptions of other provisions of the Agreement which may have impact on employment stability.

28.05 (b) The CESC shall perform the functions conferred upon it under Article 8.04 and Articles 9 and 10.

28.06 The CESC shall administer and make decisions with respect to the Joint Employment Stability Reserve Fund (JESRF), established under 28.08, by using the JESRF, or such portion as the CESC considers appropriate, to facilitate employment stability strategies, both long-term and short-term.

28.07 (a) The CESC shall make any recommendations that it is empowered to make under 28.04 and 28.05 and any decisions that it is empowered to make under 28.06 by majority vote, subject to (b) and (c) hereinafter provided. The decision of the CESC under 28.06 shall be final and binding on the parties and any employee affected by the decision. In making any decision under 28.06, the CESC shall have no power to alter, modify or amend any part of the Agreement nor to make any decision inconsistent therewith.

28.07 (b) Where there is no majority decision with respect to any recommendation under 28.04 or 28.05, each of the members of the CESC may make separate recommendations.

28.07 (c) (i) Where there is no majority decision under 28.06, any member of the CESC may refer the matter to the Employment Stability Reserve Fund Arbitrator (ESRFA), as hereinafter provided.

(ii) There shall be an Employment Stability Reserve Fund Arbitrator established at each College to be appointed by agreement of the President of the College and the President of the Union Local. The appointment, which may be renewable by mutual agreement, shall be for one (1) year, commencing on September 1 and expiring on August 31 in each year. In the event that the President of the College and the President of the Union Local are unable to agree upon the appointment of an ESRFA, either the College or the Union Local may request the College Relations Commission

APPENDIX IV

to appoint an ESRFA and the ESRFA shall, upon appointment by the College Relations Commission, have the same powers as if the appointment had been made by the College and the Union Local as provided herein.

(iii) The ESRFA may make any decision that the CESC is empowered to make under 28.06.

(iv) The ESRFA shall determine appropriate procedure and shall issue a decision within ten (10) calendar days of the referral of the matter to the ESRFA.

The ESRFA shall hear the representations of the parties and shall adopt the most expeditious and informal procedure possible.

(v) The decision of the ESRFA shall be final and binding on the parties and any employee affect by the decision. The ESRFA shall have no power to alter, modify or amend any part of the Agreement nor to make any decision inconsistent therewith.

(vi) The College and the Union shall each pay one-half of the fees and expenses of the ESRFA.

28.08 (a) There shall be established at each College a Joint Employment Stability Reserve Fund (JESRF).

28.08(b) The College shall make an annual contribution to the JESRF, to be made on or before September 1 in each year, in an amount equal to $50 per full-time member of the bargaining unit at the College, provided that where the amount of the JESRF is equal to or exceeds an amount equal to $500 per full-time member of the bargaining unit at the College, the obligation of the College to contribute to the JESRF shall be suspended until the JESRF is again below that amount. In such a case, the next annual contribution required by the College shall again be $50 per full-time member of the bargaining unit at the College or the amount required to restore the JESRF to $500 per full-time member, whichever is less.

28.08 (c) The JESRF shall be maintained at a bank or

other financial institution at which the College maintains one or more of its accounts, and shall be maintained under the supervision of the chief financial officer of the College. The books and records of the JESRF shall be open for inspection by any member of the CESC at any time during regular business hours.

28.08 (d) Any requisition for a cheque and/or withdrawal from an account in which the JESRF is maintained shall be countersigned by one member of the CESC appointed by the College and one member appointed by the Union Local.

28.08 (e) Surplus funds, if any, that are not immediately required for the purposes of 28.06 may be invested on the instructions of the CESC in any account or certificate of deposit maintained at or issued by a bank or financial institution.

28.08 (f) While it is recognized that the specific financial obligation by the College to the JESRF is the annual contribution to the JESRF (subject, in addition, to any other specific obligations imposed by the Agreement), it is understood that this is not to act as a limitation on either the College's or the Union Local's ability to explore and utilize other means of enhancing employment stability, including contributing additional funds to the JESRF.

8. TECHNOLOGICAL CHANGE

10.01 This provision shall apply when the College introduces new technology in the form of new equipment or process substantially different in nature or design from that previously in effect which has the initial effect of displacing an employee from the employee's position or more than one employee from their positions.

10.02 In such circumstances as in Article 10.01 above, the College will provide the Union Local and the College

Employment Stability Committee (CESC) at least ninety (90) calendar days before the date on which the technological change is introduced with a description of the change and the appropriate number of employees likely to be directly affected by the change. The CESC shall meet to discuss the effect on the employment status of employees directly affected and possible measures to reduce adverse effects of the technological change including discussion of developmental opportunities for employees for possible assignment to other positions within the College or assisting in a change of career for employees with suitable qualifications.

10.03 The CESC may have other persons at its meetings to assist in examination of the circumstances regarding the technological change.

10.04 The CESC may make recommendations on the measures for developmental opportunities or possibilities of other assignments, or other measures to assist the College and employees affected by the technological change.

10.05 Following the effective date of the technological change a reduction of employees resulting therefrom shall be carried out pursuant to Articles 8.04 (g) and 8.05 of this Agreement.

10.06 Where it is considered mutually desirable that the Union Local and the College set out in writing the measures to be applied such resolution shall be signed by the parties and shall have the effect of a provision of this Collective Agreement and be subject to the provisions of Article 11; but shall not however continue beyond the terms of this Agreement as currently in effect.

Appendix V

**AGREEMENT
BETWEEN
CANADA POST CORPORATION
AND THE
CANADIAN UNION OF POSTAL WORKERS**

**POSTAL OPERATIONS GROUP
(NON-SUPERVISORY)
INTERNAL MAIL PROCESSING AND
COMPLEMENTARY POSTAL SERVICES**

13.13 Acquiring Knowledge

In the application of clauses 13.07 and 13.08, it is understood that the employee must, in order to return his position, acquire the specific knowledge requirements of the job within a reasonable period of time not to exceed six (6) months.

Where the employee does not acquire the specific knowledge, he shall, as the case may be, return to his former class and, in all cases, shall be offered another position in accordance with the order of priority outlined in clause 13.07.

13.18 Bilingual Positions

(a) Effective on the date of the decision of the mediator-arbitrator, the employee who is the incumbent of a position when such position is designated as bilingual must be or become bilingual. Incumbents who are not bilingual shall be given a reasonable period of time to become bilingual. Incumbents failing to become bilingual shall be offered a non-bilingual position in accordance with the order of priority in clauses 13.07 and 13.08.

(b) Where a bilingual position becomes vacant or when a vacant position is designated bilingual it shall be filled in accordance with this agreement and in such a case the provisions of clause 13.13 shall apply provided sufficient and adequate training in the other official language has been given to the employee.

27.01 Education Leave

Upon the request of an employee, leave of absence without pay may be granted for educational purposes up to a maximum of three (3) years. Such leave shall not be unreasonably withheld.

29.11 Protection of Employees

In order to render effective the principle established in clause 29.02, the Corporation agrees to the following provisions, which are designed to protect all employees covered by this Collective Agreement:

(d) Retraining

Any employee either voluntarily or compulsorily reassigned or reclassified as a result of these changes shall be provided with whatever amount of retraining he requires during his hours of work with full pay from the Corporation and at no additional cost to the employee. Any employee unable to follow a retraining course shall maintain his classification, or its equivalent, in the bargaining unit.

31.01 Training

(a) In addition to the training provided for in Article 40, the Corporation agrees to provide a minimum of two (2) weeks' theoretical and/or practical training within a three (3) month period before assigning a new wicket clerk to the responsibility of a wicket.

(b) When a new wicket clerk is assigned to the responsibility of a wicket, a qualified wicket clerk may be assigned to provide on-the-job guidance to the new clerk and, for this purpose, the qualified wicket clerk shall then be relieved of his normal duties.

33.02 Corporation's Obligations

(b) Without limiting the generality of the foregoing, the Corporation shall:

    (iii) inform employees adequately regarding the risks relating to their work, and provide appropriate training and supervision so that the employees have the skills and knowledge necessary to safely perform the work assigned to them.

ARTICLE 40: TRAINING

40.01 Definition

For the purpose of this Agreement, "training" means any theoretical and/or practical training given by the Corporation with a view to enabling the employees to perform effectively a function, a duty or a set of functions and duties.

Cooperative Learning And Social Change
Selected Writings of Célestin Freinet
Edited and Translated by David Clandfield and John Sivell

Célestin Freinet (1896-1966) was a pioneer, an extraordinary teacher who is virtually unknown in the English-speaking world. He spent his working life teaching in small rural elementary schools in the south of France. From this base, he founded an international movement for radical educational reform through cooperative learning.

Freinet's Modern School Movement has brought together a broad community of teachers in the practical application of his innovative classroom techniques. Much of his pedagogy is as fresh and relevant today as it was in his own time. Freinet focusses on four major fronts: the importance of creative and useful work for children learning and close observation of how they do it; a direct appreciation for the natural world; a commitment to developing appropriate technologies for the classroom; and a strong emphasis on linking school and community with the wider issues of social justice and political action.

This translation is the first to bring a broad selection of Freinet's work to an English-speaking audience.

Order Form
Please send me _____ copies of *Cooperative Learning And Social Change* @ $11.50 per copy (includes GST & shipping)

Name_____
Address_____
City_____ Prov_____ Code_____
  ❑ Cheque enclosed   ❑ VISA/Mastercard
Card No._____ Expiry date_____
Signature_____

It's Our Own Knowledge

Labour, Public Education & Skills Training

This is an insightful and hard-hitting collection looking at education and work.

"We are concerned about what happens to our children in school and to our co-workers in the workplace.

We want education and training that encourages critical thinking, not uncritical compliance with authority. We want education that is oriented to the life-long needs of people, not the immediate economic desires of employers. Our educational system's goal must not be the mirage of equality and opportunity. We want equality of results in which all people will be better able to live fulfilling and meaningful lives at home, in the community, and at work."

From the Preface

These timely papers were presented at the Ontario Federation of Labour's Conference on Education and Training: Labour Issues for the 1990s. They concentrate on the issues of destreaming, work-place and classroom training, and the roles of our schools and colleges. Contributors include: Julie Davis, John Huot, Nancy Jackson, Doug Little, George Martell, Penny Moss, Doug Noble, Jim Turk, and Gord Wilson.

Order Form

Please send me _____ copies of *It's Our Own Knowledge*
@ $11.50 per copy (includes GST & shipping)

Name_____

Address_____

City_____ Prov_____ Code_____

☐ Cheque enclosed   ☐ VISA/Mastercard

Card No._____ Expiry date_____

Signature_____

Join The Debate On What Should Happen In Canada's Schools. You Can Still Get Your Own Copy Of Each Of These Issues Of Our Schools/Our Selves.

Issue #1: (Journal) A Feminist Agenda For Canadian Education ... The Saskatoon Native Survival School ... School Wars: BC, Alberta, Manitoba ... Contracting Out At The Toronto Board ... On Strike: Toronto Teachers And Saskatoon Profs ... Labour's Message in Nova Scotia Schools and Queen's Park ... The Free Trade Ratchet ...

Issue #2: Educating Citizens: A Democratic Socialist Agenda For Canadian Education by Ken Osborne. A coherent curriculum policy focussed on "active citizenship." Osborne takes on the issues of a "working-class curriculum" and a national "core" curriculum: what should student's know about Canada and the world at large?

Issue #3: (Journal) BC Teachers, Solidarity and Vander Zalm ... The Anti-Streaming Battle in Ontario ... The Dangers of School-Based Budgeting ... "Whole Language" in Nova Scotia ... Vancouver's Elementary Schools 1920-60 ... The Martimes in Song and Text ... Teaching "G-Level" Kids ... The Squeeze on Alberta's Teachers ... In Winnipeg: "The Green Slime Strikes Back!" ...

Issue #4: (Journal) Teaching The Real Stuff Of The World: Bears, History, Work Skills ... Tory Times At Sask Ed ... The NDP At The Toronto School Board ... Indian Control In Alberta Schools ... Is The Action Affirmative For Women School Board Workers ... Radwanski: The Dark Side ... More On "Whole Language" In Nova Scotia ... A Steelworker's Education ... B.C. Teachers Hang Tough ... Decoding Discrimination ...

Issue #5: Making A People's Curriculum: The Experience Of La maîtresse d'école edited with an introduction by David Clandfield. Since 1975 this Montreal teacher collective has been producing alternative francophone curricula on labour, human rights, peace, and geopolitical issues in a framework of cooperative learning. This is an anthology of their best work.

Issue #6: (Journal) Labour Education And The Auto Workers ... Nova Scotia's Children Of The State ... Patrick Watson's *Democracy* ... Popular Roots Of The "New Literacy" ... Canada's Learner Centres ... Right Wing Thinking In Education ... Fighting Sexism In Nfld ... The Computer Bandwagon ... *Glasnost* and *Perestroika* Over Here? Funding Native Education ...

Issue #7: Claiming An Education: Feminism and Canadian Schools by Jane Gaskell, Arlene McLaren, Myra Novogrodsky. This book examines "equal opportunity," what students learn about women, what women learn about themselves and what has been accomplished by women who teach, as mothers and teachers.

Issue #8: It's Our Own Knowledge: Labour, Public Education & Skills Training by Julie Davis et al. The clearest expression yet of Labour's new educational agenda for the 1990s. It begins with working class experience in the schools and community colleges, takes issue with corporate initiatives in skills training, and proposes a program "for workers, not for bosses."

Issue #9: (Journal) Rekindling Literacy In Mozambique ... Privatizing The Community Colleges ... CUPE's Educational Agenda ... High Schools & Teenage Sex ... Workers And The Rise of Mass Schooling ... More On Nova Scotia's Children of the State ... Grade 1 Learning ... Private School Funding ... The Globe's Attack on Media Studies ... "Consolidation" in PEI ... Manitoba's High School Review ...

Issue #10: Heritage Languages: The Development And Denial Of Canada's Linguistic Resources by Jim Cummins and Marcel Danesi. This book opens up the issue of teaching heritage languages in our schools to a broad audience. It provides the historical context, analyzes opposing positions, examines the rationale and research support for heritage language promotion, and looks at the future of multiculturalism and multilingualism in Canada.

Issue #11: (Journal) No More War Toys: The Quebec Campaign ... Labelling the Under-Fives ... Building a Socialist Curriculum ... High School Streaming in Ontario ... Growing Up Male in Nova Scotia ... New Left Academics ... Tory Cutbacks in Alberta ... More On Workers And The Rise Of Mass Schooling ... The Elementary School Ruby And How High School Turned Her Sour ...

Double Issue #12-13: What Our High Schools Could Be: A Teacher's Reflections From The 60s To The 90s by Bob Davis. The author leads us where his experience has led him — as a teacher in a treatment centre for disturbed children, in an alternative community school, in a graduate education faculty, and for 23 years in two Metro Toronto high schools. The book ranges from powerful description to sharp analysis — from sex education to student streaming to the new skills mania.

Issue #14: (Journal) Feminism, Schools and the Union ... What's Happening in China's Schools ... NB Teacher Aides and the Struggle for Standards ... Barbie Dolls and Unicef ... Post-secondary Cuts in Alberta ... CUPE-Teacher Links ... Language Control In Nova Scotia ... Pay Equity For Ontario Teachers ... Women's Struggles/Men's Responsibility ...

Issue #15: Cooperative Learning And Social Change: Selected Writings Of Célestin Freinet edited and translated by David Clandfield and John Sivell. Célestin Freinet (1896-1966) pioneered an international movement for radical educational reform through cooperative learning. His pedagogy is as fresh and relevant today as it was in his own time, whether dealing with the importance of creative and useful work for children or linking schooling and community with wider issues of social justice and political action. This translation is the first to bring a broad selection of Freinet's work to an English-speaking audience.

Issue #16: (Journal) BC's Privatization Of Apprenticeship ... Marketing Adult Ed In Saskatchewan ... The Future Of Ontario's CAATs ... Edmonton's Catalyst Theatre ... The Money Crisis In Nova Scotia Schools ... The Politics Of Children's Literature ... Tough Kids Out Of Control ... A Literacy Policy For Newfoundland? ... Métis Schooldays ... Capitalism And Donald Duck ... In Struggle: Ontario Elementary Teachers ...

Issue #17: (Journal) Towards An Anti-Racist Curriculum ... Discovering Columbus ... The Baffin Writers' Project ... The Anti-Apartheid Struggle In South Africa's Schools ... What People Think About Schooling ... Children's Work ... Radical Literacy ... Getting the Gulf Into The Classroom ... Bye-Bye Minimum C Grades ... Taking Action On AIDS ...

Issue #18: (Journal) Can The NDP Make A Difference?... Columbus In Children's Literature ... Labour Takes On Ontario's Education Bureaucrats ... Lessons From Yukon Schools ... Vision 2000 Revisited ... Getting A Feminist Education The Hard Way ... Children In Poverty ... Reflections Of A Lesbian Teacher ... Literacy, Politics and Religion in Newfoundland ... Critiquing the National Indicators ... Student Loans In Saskatchewan ...

Double Issue #19-20: Teaching For Democratic Citizenship by Ken Osborne. In this book Osborne extends his work in *Educating Citizens* and takes us through the world of modern pedagogies and the most recent research on effective teaching. He focuses particularly on "discovery learning," "critical pedagogy," and "feminist pedagogy" — drawing from a wide range of classroom practice — and builds on this foundation the key elements of an approach to teaching in which democratic citizenship is the core of student experience.

Issue #21: (Journal) The Tory Agenda ... Higher Education For Sale ... Racism and Education: Fighting Back in Nova Scotia, in a Scarborough Collegiate, in South Africa and in Victoria's Chinese Student Strike ... Saskatchewan's Neo-Conservatives ... As Neutral As My Teacher, Jesus ... "Make Work" in New Brunswick ... Teachers Politics: In Ontario and Mexico ... A Feminist Presence ... Canada's Heritage Language Programs ...

Issue #22: Their Rightful Place: An Essay On Children, Families and Childcare in Canada by Loren Lind and Susan Prentice. The authors examine the complex ways we view our children in both private and public life and the care we give them inside our families and within a network of private and public childcare. They also offer an historical perspective on families and childcare in Canada and propose a strategy to develop "a free, universally accessible, publicly-funded, non-compulsory, high quality, non-profit, community-based childcare system" right across the country.

Issue #23: (Journal) Corporate Visions ... Taking on the Montreal School Commission ... Postmodern Literacy ... A Neo-Conservative Agenda in Manitoba ... Facing up to High School Sexism ... Education in the Age of Ecology ... An Autoworkers' Education Agenda ... Learning About Work ... The Politics of Literacy ...

Issue #24: Stacking The Deck: The Streaming Of Working Class Kids In Ontario Schools by Bruce Curtis, D.W. Livingstone & Harry Smaller. This book examines the history and structure of class bias in Ontario education. It looks at both elementary and secondary schooling and proposes a new deal for working class children. The evidence is taken from the Ontario system, but the ideas and analysis can be extended to every school in Canada.

Issue #25: (Journal) The Meaning Of Yonge Street ... What Should The NDP Do? ... New Brunswick's Plunge Into 'Excellence' ... Bargaining For Childcare ... Denmark's Efterskoles ... Reader Response And Postmodern Literacy ... Against Skills ... Slash And Burn In Nova Scotia Schools ...

Subscribe Today, And Give A Subscription To A Friend.

Here's What's Coming In Future Issues Of Our Schools/Our Selves

Articles On:

What Do We Tell Our Kids About Canada — Science And Standardized Testing — Environmental Activism — Unionizing ESL Teachers — A Winnipeg Inner City School — CUPE's Fight For Parental Leave — The Nuclear Agenda in Saskatchewan Schools — Bilingual Education — The World Of Teenage Girls — The BC School Wars Continue — Labour, Education And The Arts — Young Women In Trades — Education Politics In Alberta — Inside The Labelling Process — Schools And Museums — Ninja Turtles — Mi'kmaq Language Policy

You'll get three journals and three books a year for each subscription.

Books On:

Labour And Technical Education — Getting A Feminist Education The Hard Way — The Corporate Agenda In Canadian Education — A Socialist-Feminist Approach To Phys Ed — What Happened To High School History? — Democracy And Schools — Native Control Of White Education — Assessment And Evaluation — Australian Education Activism — The Politics Of Reading And Writing — A Democratic Socialist Approach To Whole Language — Teaching History — What Do People Really Think About Education? — An NDP Agenda — An Anti-Racist Curriculum For Nova Scotia Schools — Sex In Schools — Media Studies

It's a great bargain, as much as 50% off the newstand price.